μ

VIKING
GODS AND
HEROES

VIKING
GODS AND
HEROES

E. M. WILMOT-BUXTON

DOVER PUBLICATIONS, INC.
Mineola, New York

Bibliographical Note

This Dover edition, first published in 2004, is an unabridged republication of the text of *Told By the Northmen: Stories from the Eddas and Sagas,* originally published by George G. Harrap & Co. Ltd., London, in 1908.

Library of Congress Cataloging-in-Publication Data

Wilmot-Buxton, E. M. (Ethel Mary)
    [Told by the Northmen]
    Viking gods and heroes / E.M. Wilmot-Buxton.
      p. cm.
    Originally published: Told by the Northmen. London : G.G. Harrap, 1908.
    Summary: A collection of myths about Thor, Odin, Sigurd, and other Nordic gods, goddesses, and heroes.
    ISBN 0-486-43704-3 (pbk.)
    1. Mythology, Norse—Juvenile literature. [1. Mythology, Norse.] I. Title.

BL860.W46 2004
398.2'09481'01—dc22

2004049315

Manufactured in the United States by Courier Corporation
43704302
www.doverpublications.com

Contents

Hakon's Lay

By James Russell Lowell

"O Skald, sing now an olden song,
  Such as our fathers heard who led great lives;
  And, as the bravest on a shield is borne
  Along the waving host that shouts him king,
  So rode their thrones upon the thronging seas!"

Then the old man arose: white-haired he stood,
  White-bearded, and with eyes that looked afar
  From their still region of perpetual snow,
  Over the little smokes and stirs of men:
  His head was bowed with gathered flakes of years,
  As winter bends the sea-foreboding pine,
  But something triumphed in his brow and eye,
  Which whoso saw it, could not see and crouch:
  Loud rang the emptied beakers as he mused,
  Brooding his eyried thoughts; then, as an eagle
  Circles smooth-winged above the wind-vexed woods,
  So wheeled his soul into the air of song
  High o'er the stormy hall; and thus he sang:

"The fletcher for his arrow-shaft picks out
  Wood closest-grained, long-seasoned, straight as light;
  And, from a quiver full of such as these,
  The wary bow-man, matched against his peers,
  Long doubting, singles yet once more the best.
  Who is it that can make such shafts as Fate?
  What archer of his arrows is so choice,
  Or hits the white so surely? They are men,
  The chosen of her quiver; nor for her
  Will every reed suffice, or cross-grained stick
  At random from life's vulgar fagot plucked:
  Such answer household ends; but she will have
  Souls straight and clear, of toughest fibre, sound

Down to the heart of heat; from these she strips
All needless stuff, all sapwood; hardens them,
From circumstance untoward feathers plucks
Crumpled and cheap, and barbs with iron will:
The hour that passes is her quiver-boy;
When she draws bow, 'tis not across the wind,
Nor 'gainst the sun, her haste-snatched arrow sings,
For sun and wind have plighted faith to her:
Ere men have heard the sinew twang, behold,
In the butt's heart her trembling messenger!

"The song is old and simple that I sing:
Good were the days of yore, when men were tried
By ring of shields, as now by ring of gold;
But, while the gods are left, and hearts of men,
And the free ocean, still the days are good;
Through the broad Earth roams Opportunity
And knocks at every door of hut or hall,
Until she finds the brave soul that she wants."

He ceased, and instantly the frothy tide
Of interrupted wassail roared along.

VIKING
GODS AND
HEROES

CHAPTER I

How All Things Began

ONCE upon a time, before ever this world was made, there was neither earth nor sea, nor air, nor light, but only a great yawning gulf, full of twilight, where these things should be.

To the north of this gulf lay the Home of Mist, a dark and dreary land, out of which flowed a river of water from a spring that never ran dry. As the water in its onward course met the bitter blasts of wind from the yawning gulf, it hardened into great blocks of ice, which rolled far down into the abyss with a thunderous roar and piled themselves one on another until they formed mountains of glistening ice.

South of this gulf lay the Home of Fire, a land of burning heat, guarded by a giant with a flaming sword which, as he flashed it to and fro before the entrance, sent forth showers of sparks. And these sparks fell upon the ice-blocks and partly melted them, so that they sent up clouds of steam; and these again were frozen into hoar-frost, which filled all the space that was left in the midst of the mountains of ice.

Then one day, when the gulf was full to the very top, this great mass of frosty rime, warmed by the flames from the Home of Fire and frozen by the cold airs from the Home of Mist, came to life and became the Giant Ymir, with a living, moving body and cruel heart of ice.

Now there was as yet no tree, nor grass, nor anything that would serve for food, in this gloomy abyss. But when the Giant Ymir began to grope around for something to satisfy his hunger, he heard a sound as of some animal chewing the cud; and there among the ice-hills he saw a gigantic cow, from whose udder flowed four great streams of milk, and with this his craving was easily stilled.

But the cow was hungry also, and began to lick the salt off the blocks of ice by which she was surrounded. And presently, as she went on licking with her strong, rough tongue, a head of hair pushed itself through the melting ice. Still the cow went on licking, until she had at last melted all the icy covering and there stood fully revealed the frame of a mighty man.

Ymir looked with eyes of hatred at this being, born of snow and ice, for somehow he knew that his heart was warm and kind, and that he and his sons would always be the enemies of the evil race of the Frost Giants.

So, indeed, it came to pass. For from the sons of Ymir came a race of giants whose pleasure was to work evil on the earth; and from the Sons of the Iceman sprang the race of the gods, chief of whom was Odin, Father of All Things that ever were made; and Odin and his brothers began at once to war against the wicked Frost Giants, and most of all against the cold-hearted Ymir, whom in the end they slew.

Now when, after a hard fight, the Giant Ymir was slain, such a river of blood flowed forth from his wounds that it drowned all the rest of the Frost Giants save one, who escaped in a boat, with only his wife on board, and sailed away to the edge of the world. And from him sprang all the new race of Frost Giants, who at every opportunity issued from their land of twilight and desolation to harm the gods in their abode of bliss.

Now when the giants had been thus driven out, All-Father Odin set to work with his brothers to make the earth, the sea, and the sky; and these they fashioned out of the great body of the Giant Ymir.

Out of his flesh they formed Midgard, the earth, which lay in the centre of the gulf; and all round it they planted his eyebrows to make a high fence which should defend it from the race of giants.

With his bones they made the lofty hills, with his teeth the cliffs, and his thick curly hair took root and became trees, bushes, and the green grass.

With his blood they made the ocean, and his great skull, poised aloft, became the arching sky. Just below this they scattered his brains, and made of them the heavy grey clouds that lie between earth and heaven.

The sky itself was held in place by four strong dwarfs, who support it on their broad shoulders as they stand east and west and south and north.

The next thing was to give light to the new-made world. So the gods caught sparks from the Home of Fire and set them in the sky for stars; and they took the living flame and made of it the sun and moon, which they placed in chariots of gold, and harnessed to them beautiful horses, with flowing manes of gold and silver. Before the horses of the sun, they placed a mighty shield to protect them from its hot rays; but the swift moon steeds needed no such protection from its gentle heat.

And now all was ready save that there was no one to drive the horses of the sun and moon. This task was given to Mani and Sol, the beautiful son and daughter of a giant; and these fair charioteers drive their fleet steeds along the paths marked out by the gods, and not only give light to the earth but mark out months and days for the sons of men.

Then All-Father Odin called forth Night, the gloomy daughter of the cold-hearted giant folk, and set her to drive the dark chariot drawn by the black horse, Frosty-Mane, from whose long wavy hair the drops of dew and hoar-frost fall upon the earth below. After her drove her radiant son, Day, with his white steed Shining-Mane, from whom the bright beams of daylight shine forth to gladden the hearts of men.

But the wicked giants were very angry when they saw all these good things; and they set in the sky two hungry wolves, that the fierce, grey creatures might for ever pursue the sun and moon, and devour them, and so bring all things to an end. Sometimes, indeed, or so say the men of the North, the grey wolves almost succeed in swallowing sun or moon; and then the earth children make such an uproar that the fierce beasts drop their prey in fear. And the sun and moon flee more rapidly than before, still pursued by the hungry monsters.

One day, so runs the tale, as Mani, the Man in the Moon, was hastening on his course, he gazed upon the earth and saw two beautiful little children, a boy and a girl, carrying between them a pail of water. They looked very tired and sleepy, and indeed they were, for a cruel giant made them fetch and carry water all night long, when they should have been in bed. So Mani put out a long, long arm and snatched up the children and set them in the moon, pail and all; and there you can see them on any moonlight night for yourself.

But that happened a long time after the beginning of things; for as yet there was no man or woman or child upon the earth.

And now that this pleasant Midgard was made, the gods determined to satisfy their desire for an abode where they might rest and enjoy themselves in their hours of ease.

They chose a suitable place far above the earth, on the other side of the great river which flowed from the Home of Mist where the giants dwelt, and here they made for their abode Asgard, wherein they dwelt in peace and happiness, and from whence they could look down upon the sons of men.

From Asgard to Midgard they built a beautiful bridge of many colours, to which men gave the name of Rainbow Bridge, and up and down which the gods could pass on their journeys to and from the earth.

Here in Asgard stood the mighty forge where the gods fashioned their weapons wherewith they fought the giants, and the tools wherewith they built their palaces of gold and silver.

Meantime, no human creature lived upon the earth, and the giants dared not cross its borders for fear of the gods. But one of them, clad in eagles' plumes, always sat at the north side of Midgard, and, whenever he raised his arms and let them fall again, an icy blast rushed forth from the Mist Home and nipped all the pleasant things of earth with its cruel breath. In due time the earth was no longer without life, for the ground brought forth thousands of tiny creatures, which crawled about and showed signs of great intelligence. And when the gods examined these little people closely, they found that they were of two kinds.

Some were ugly, misshapen, and cunning-faced, with great heads, small bodies, long arms and feet. These they called Trolls or Dwarfs or Gnomes, and sent them to live underground, threatening to turn them into stone should they appear in the daytime. And this is why the trolls spend all their time in the hidden parts of the earth, digging for gold and silver and precious stones, and hiding their spoil away in secret holes and corners. Sometimes they blow their tiny fires and set to work to make all kinds of wonderful things from this buried treasure;

and that is what they are doing when, if one listens very hard on the mountains and hills of the Northland, a sound of tap-tap-tapping is heard far underneath the ground.

The other small earth creatures were very fair and light and slender, kindly of heart, and full of goodwill. These the gods called Fairies or Elves, and gave to them a charming place called Elfland in which to dwell. Elfland lies between Asgard and Midgard, and since all fairies have wings they can easily flit down to the earth to play with the butterflies, teach the young birds to sing, water the flowers, or dance in the moonlight round a fairy ring.

Last of all, the gods made a man and woman to dwell in fair Midgard; and this is the manner of their creation.

All-Father Odin was walking with his brothers in Midgard where, by the seashore, they found growing two trees, an ash and an elm. Odin took these trees and breathed on them, whereupon a wonderful transformation took place. Where the trees had stood, there were a living man and woman, but they were stupid, pale, and speechless, until Hœnir, the god of Light, touched their foreheads and gave them sense and wisdom; and Loki, the Fire-god, smoothed their faces, giving them bright colour and warm blood, and the power to speak and see and hear. It only remained that they should be named, and they were called Ask and Embla, the names of the trees from which they had been formed. From these two people sprang all the race of men which lives upon this earth.

And now All-Father Odin completed his work by planting the Tree of Life.

This immense tree had its roots in Asgard and Midgard and the Mist Land; and it grew to such a marvellous height that the highest bough, the Bough of Peace, hung over the Hall of Odin on the heights of Asgard; and the other branches overshadowed both Midgard and the Mist Land. On the top of the Peace Bough was perched a mighty eagle, and ever a falcon sat between his eyes, and kept watch on all that happened in the world below, that he might tell to Odin what he saw.

Heidrun, the goat of Odin, who supplied the heavenly mead, browsed on the leaves of this wonderful tree, and from them fed also the four mighty stags from whose horns honey-dew dropped on to the earth beneath and supplied water for all the rivers of Midgard.

The leaves of the Tree of Life were ever green and fair, despite the dragon which, aided by countless serpents, gnawed perpetually at its roots, in order that they might kill the Tree of Life and thus bring about the destruction of the gods.

Up and down the branches of the tree scampered the squirrel, Ratatosk, a malicious little creature, whose one amusement it was to make mischief by repeating to the eagle the rude remarks of the dragon, and to the dragon those of the eagle, in the hope that one day he might see them in actual conflict.

Near the roots of the Tree of Life is a sacred well of sweet water from which the three Weird Sisters, who know all that shall come to pass, sprinkle the tree and keep it fresh and green. And the water, as it trickles down from the leaves, falls as drops of honey on the earth, and the bees take it for their food.

Close to this sacred well is the Council Hall of the gods, to which every morning they rode, over the Rainbow Bridge, to hold converse together.

And this is the end of the tale of How All Things began.

CHAPTER II

How All-Father Odin Became Wise

These are the tales which the Northmen tell concerning the wisdom of All-Father Odin

ON the highest hill of Asgard, upon a great chair, sat All-Father Odin, watching from thence all that was happening on and above and under the earth.

The Father of Asas and of men had long grey locks and thick curling beard, and he wore a great blue coat flecked with grey like unto the sky when the fleecy clouds scud across it.

In his hand he carried a spear, so sacred that, if anyone swore an oath upon its point, that oath could never be broken.

On his head he wore, when sitting upon his watch-tower throne, a helmet shaped like an eagle; but when he wandered, as he loved to do, about the earth, he wore a large broad-brimmed hat drawn low over his forehead.

Perched on his broad shoulders sat two inky-black ravens, Hugin and Munin, whom every morning he sent to wing their flight about the world that they might see what was going on.

Every evening when they returned, they whispered all that they had seen and heard in his ears.

At Odin's feet crouched two great wolves, whom he fed from the meat set before him; for he himself cared not to eat flesh-food, and preferred rather to drink the sacred mead provided by the goat who fed upon the leaves of the Tree of Life.

Sometimes Odin left his watch-tower throne for the great Council Hall where the twelve Asas sat and took counsel together; but his favourite seat of all was in his own palace of Valhalla, or the Hall of the Chosen Slain. This palace stood in the midst of a wonderful grove of trees, whose leaves were all of red gold, rustling and shimmering in the breeze. Five and forty doors opened into it, each wide enough to allow eight hundred warriors to enter abreast, and over the chief entrance was a boar's head and a great eagle, whose keen gaze looked forth over all the world. The walls of the palace were built of spears of polished steel, so bright that they lighted the whole building; and the roof was made of golden shields.

> "And wondrous gleamed Valhalla on the heights,—
> Her walls shone bright as rows of glittering spears;
> The roof resplendent like great golden shields;
> Hundreds of open gates and welcoming doors
> For myriad warriors from the fields of earth,—
> The chosen heroes of the future years,
> To be great Odin's mighty bodyguard
> Against the awful prophecies of doom."

From end to end of the great hall stood long tables and benches loaded with armour, ready prepared for the fortunate guests. And this was the manner of their selection. Whenever a great battle was about to be fought on the earth, Odin sent forth the nine Valkyrs, or Battle Maidens, his especial attendants, to watch the progress of the fight and to choose from the fallen warriors half of their number. These the Battle Maidens carried on their swift steeds over the Rainbow Bridge into the great hall of Valhalla, where they were welcomed by the sons of Odin and and taken to the All-Father's throne to receive his greeting. But if one had shown himself especially heroic in the fight, Odin would descend from his throne and advance to the door to bid him welcome.

And now, seated at the long tables, loaded with great beakers of mead and dishes of boar flesh, the warriors feasted merrily, tended by the fair Battle Maidens.

> "The blazing roof resounds
> The genial uproar of those shades who fall
> In desperate fight, or by some brave attempt."

When they had eaten all they could, the warriors would call for their weapons, ride out into the great courtyard, and there wage desperate fights, in the course of which many a man would be sorely wounded. But this mattered little, for at the sound of the dinner horn all wounds were healed.

> "And all day long they there are hacked and hewn
> 'Mid dust, and groans, and limbs lopped off, and blood
> But all at night return to Odin's hall
> Woundless and fresh; such lot is theirs in heaven."

These warriors were Odin's special joy and delight, and he was never weary of watching them at feast or in the combat. Sometimes, indeed, when some battle on earth was impending, he would appear, riding upon his eight-footed grey horse, and with white shield on arm would fling his glittering spear into the ranks of the warriors as signal for the fight to begin, and would rush into the fray with his war-cry, "Odin has you all!"

Now, though all this shows very clearly that All-Father Odin was a warlike Asa and delighted in battles, there was another side to his character, for beyond all the other Asas he cared for wisdom.

Very early in the morn of time All-Father Odin discovered that beneath the roots of the Tree of Life, just where sky and ocean met, there was a marvellous spring of water, "the fountain of all wit and wisdom." Looking into its crystal depths, all that was going to happen in the future was revealed, and anyone drinking of it received the gifts of wisdom, knowledge, and right judgment about all things. Now this spring was guarded by the

Giant Mimir, who prided himself upon being wiser than any other giants or Asas could be, for he alone had the right to draw water from the well; and every morning, dipping his glittering horn therein, he drank a long draught, and with every draught he grew wiser, till he knew everything that was past and present and is to come.

When Odin became aware of the marvellous properties of the spring, he was eager to drink of it, "for," said he, "it is not fitting that a giant should know more than the Father of Asas and men."

So early one morn he entered a dark grove of trees, where, amidst great arching roots fantastically intertwined, bubbled the spring; and keeping watch beside it sat Giant Mimir, his long grey beard sweeping over his knees, and his great piercing eyes shining with fierce light as the new-comer approached.

"What do you want here?" he demanded, in a voice that sounded like the muttering of thunder before a storm.

"I want a drink of yon water from your glittering horn, good Mimir," said Odin.

But Giant Mimir sunk his great head upon his chest, and looking from under his shaggy eyebrows, growled again:

"Begone, I tell you. I give no man drink from my well."

Then Odin drew himself up to his full height, and in a voice that was more thunderous than that of the giant himself, cried:

"No man am I, O Mimir, but Odin, Father of Asas and men. Refuse not to me the gift of wisdom; for though I can see all things that happen in heaven and earth, I cannot see what lies beneath the deep, nor can I see what shall happen in the future. Give me, therefore, the draught of wisdom, and I will pay you whatsoever you demand."

But Mimir still refused. "We giants are of elder race than ye Asas be," he said, "and all the wisdom in the world is in our hands. If I give you to drink of this water you will become wise even as we are, and an enemy more dangerous than ever."

"Nevertheless," replied Odin firmly, "you must give me the water, and I will pay you whatsoever you may ask."

Then Mimir, feeling sure that such a payment would be refused, said, "I will give you the magic draught in return for one of your eyes."

But to his amazement, for the god was very proud of his keen vision, Odin at once plucked forth an eye and handed it to him, saying:

"No price is too high to pay for wisdom."

So Mimir was obliged to hand him the horn filled with precious water, and Odin drank a full draught, caring not at all that henceforth he was to have but one eye, for he knew that he had gained the precious gift of wisdom beyond any in the world save Mimir himself.

Meantime, Mimir dropped the eye of the Asa into the well, where it shines bright as the moon reflected in still waters; and he bade Odin depart, saying heavily, "This day is the beginning of trouble betwixt your race and mine."

Determined to put his new-found wisdom to the test, All-Father Odin now disguised himself as a wandering minstrel and went to visit the Most Learned of all the Giants save Mimir, who, of course, knew everything in the whole world. And the Most Learned Giant received him graciously, and consented readily to enter into a contest of wit, and it was agreed that the loser should forfeit his head.

The Most Learned Giant was the first to begin. He questioned Odin as to the size and colour of the horses which bore the chariots of Night and Day across the sky; he asked him the source of the river which separated the Land of the Giants from Asgard, and finally he demanded details about the last battle that was to be fought between Asas and giants in far-distant days.

All these questions were fully and promptly answered by Odin, and it was now his turn. He questioned his rival first as to the Beginning of All Things; then he asked what the heroes did in Valhalla, what was the work of the Weird Sisters, and who would carry on the work of the gods when they had passed away.

And all these were fully answered by the Most Learned Giant.

Then Odin bent down to the Giant's ear as he sat on his great seat, and said softly:

"Tell me, lastly, I pray you, what are the words that the All-Father will whisper to his son Balder as he lies dead upon his funeral pyre?"

At this the Most Learned Giant uprose, and looking hard into the sad and troubled face of his questioner, said:

"No one but Odin himself can answer that question, and no

one but Odin would have asked it. For only he who has drunk of the water of wisdom would foresee the death in the far-off future of his dearest son. Kill me now, therefore, for thou hast triumphed."

Here the tale comes to an end; but we should like to think that Odin spared the life of the Most Learned Giant, and perhaps he would have done so the more readily because his heart was softened by the knowledge, born of his new-found wisdom, that Balder, his beautiful son, must die.

Another story is told in which Odin's great wisdom seemed for a time at fault.

We have noticed how fond was the All-Father of watching the affairs of mortal men. He was especially interested, at one time, in two handsome little princes, the sons of a certain king, who were usually to be found playing or wrestling or riding together on the seashore which bounded their father's kingdom.

Geirrod and Agnar were the names of these boys, and All-Father Odin and his wife Frigga grew so fond of them both that, disguising themselves as an old man and woman, they went to live upon a desert island which lay far out at sea, opposite the beach where the children played. Presently it came to pass, exactly as they hoped, that the boys went fishing, and Odin made a storm to arise, and the rough wind blew the little boat away from the land, and finally stranded it upon the island.

The boys, frightened, wet, and hungry, came timidly to the door of the hut where the old people dwelt and asked for shelter. They were received kindly by Odin and Frigga, who kept the boys all the long winter, making much of them and delighting in their childish fun and merriment. Geirrod was Odin's favourite. He taught him to fight, to swim, and to use the bow and spear. But Frigga loved best the gentle little Agnar, the elder boy, who would sit by her side and rest his head upon her knee, well contented, while she told him strange tales of beautiful Asgard, the home of the gods.

Spring came at length, and, when the sea was calm and still, Odin put the two boys aboard a boat and bade them sail back to their father. And Agnar grieved at leaving his kind old friends, but Geirrod did not even so much as look back to respond to their farewell.

The favourable breezes which Odin had called up soon urged the boat to land; but the moment it touched the shore Geirrod sprang out, and, pushing it back into the sea with all his might, bade his brother sail away to the Land of Giants and never return.

Odin, feeling sure that all was well with the boys, had resigned his care for their safety and had returned to Asgard, and thus the giants were able to play him a trick, which they did by causing the wind to veer round, whereby Agnar was carried away to the edge of the world.

Meantime, the hard-hearted Geirrod ran cheerfully into his father's palace, and announced that he had come back alone from a desert island upon which his boat had been stranded, his elder brother having been drowned in the sea.

His father was overjoyed to see him, for he had given up hope of setting eyes on either of his sons again. He made him his heir, and in due time, when some years had passed away, he died, and Geirrod became king in his stead.

Now All-Father Odin had so many things to attend to that, as we have seen, he thought no more of his boy friends for many years.

Then at length, when Geirrod had sat for some time on his father's throne, Odin looked from his high seat in Asgard upon him, and seeing with pleasure how great a man he had become, his thoughts turned to Agnar. For a time he could see nothing of him, but at last he discerned that he had returned in disguise to his brother's palace and was living there, unknown to Geirrod, as a servant.

Then Odin turned to Frigga, who sat by his side on the high seat, and said tauntingly, "Did I not always say that Geirrod was by far the better and braver and stronger of those two boys? Behold, although he is the younger, he sits upon his father's throne, while Agnar brews ale for his table."

To this Frigga quietly replied: "It is better to be a poor servant than a hard-hearted king. For see how rich is Geirrod; yet he turns away the guest from the door, and ill-treats those who ask a kindness at his hands."

"I will never believe it," said Odin, who could be very obstinate when he liked; "and to prove you are wrong I will disguise myself again as a wanderer, and ask for food and shelter from the king."

So he took his blue-grey cloak and broad-brimmed hat, and,

with a pilgrim's staff in his hand, set off adown the Rainbow Bridge. Meantime, Frigga, determined to show that she was right, and to prevent Geirrod from receiving Odin with favour by mere chance, sent a swift and secret messenger, warning the king to beware of a man in a blue-grey mantle and wide-brimmed hat, for that he, a pretended wanderer, was an enchanter who would put the king under a spell.

Scarcely had the messenger fulfilled his mission when Odin knocked at the great door of the palace and begged for food and shelter. He had not the slightest doubt that these would be granted him, for inhospitality to strangers was one of the greatest crimes a Northman could commit.

Judge then of his surprise when, instead of being offered a seat at the supper-table and a bed for the night, he was seized by the beard, and dragged roughly into the presence of Geirrod.

"Where do you come from, and what is your name, O miserable old man?" asked the angry king.

"My name is Grimnir," answered Odin, now well on his guard, "but where I come from I will not say, since that is my concern alone."

Then the king's wrath knew no bounds, and finding it impossible to make the old man speak, he ordered that he should be chained to a pillar between two fires, whose flames scorched him on either side without actually burning him.

For eight days and nights was Odin imprisoned thus, and during all that time the cruel Geirrod would give him neither food nor drink, and kept close watch to see that he obtained them from no one else.

But one night, when the watchmen were drowsy from the heat of the fire, a serving-man came stealthily over the floor, a horn of ale in his hand. Holding this to the parched lips of the prisoner, he gave him a long, cool drink; and then did Odin recognize the features of Agnar, brother of the king, who should have been king in his stead.

The next evening, as Geirrod sat at the head of the table gloating over the sufferings of his prisoner, Odin suddenly began to sing. Softly the notes began, but soon they grew louder and louder, till the great hall echoed and re-echoed the song of triumph. And at length he sang how Geirrod, who had so long enjoyed the favour of the gods, was now about to meet the just reward of his misdeeds:

> "Thy life is now run out:
> Wroth with thee are the gods:
> Odin thou now shalt see:
> Draw near me if thou canst."

With these words the chain fell from off his hands, the flames shot up to the roof and died away, and Odin stood in the midst of the hall, no longer a poor and suffering wayfarer, but revealed in all the might and majesty of a god.

Directly he had understood the meaning of the song, Geirrod had risen to his feet with drawn sword, meaning to kill his prisoner, but so startled was he at the sudden change in his appearance that he stumbled back, and, losing his footing, he fell upon the sharp point of his own sword and miserably perished.

When his words had been thus fulfilled, Odin turned to Agnar, who, with the other servants, had rushed into the hall, and bade him take his rightful place upon his father's throne, and in return for his kind act in bringing the draught of ale he promised him prosperity and happiness so long as he should live.

CHAPTER III

How the Queen of the Sky Gave Gifts to Men

This is the tale which the Northmen tell of Frigga, Queen of the Asas

B Y the side of All-Father Odin, upon his high seat in Asgard, sat Frigga, his wife, the Queen of the Asas. Sometimes she would be dressed in snow-white garments, bound at the waist by a golden girdle, from which hung a great bunch of golden keys. And the earth-dwellers, gazing into the sky, would admire the great white clouds as they floated across the blue, not perceiving that these clouds were really the folds of Frigga's flowing white robe, as it waved in the wind.

At other times she would wear dark grey or purple garments; and then the earth-dwellers made haste into their houses, for they said, "the sky is lowering to-day, and a storm is nigh at hand."

Frigga had a palace of her own called Fensalir, or the Hall of Mists, where she spent much of her time at her wheel, spinning golden thread, or weaving web after web of many-coloured clouds. All night long she sat at this golden wheel, and if you look at the sky on a starry night you may chance to see it set up where the men of the South show a constellation called the Girdle of Orion.

Husbands and wives who had dwelt lovingly together upon earth were invited by Frigga to her hall when they died, so that they might be for ever united within its hospitable walls.

> "There in the glen Fensalir stands, the house
> Of Frigga, honoured mother of the gods,
> And shows its lighted windows, and the open doors."

Frigga was especially interested in all good housewives, and she herself set them an excellent example in Fensalir. When the snowflakes fell, the earth-dwellers knew it was Frigga shaking her great feather bed, and when it rained they said it was her washing day. It was she who first gave to them the gift of flax that the women upon earth might spin, and weave, and bleach their linen as white as the clouds of her own white robe.

And this is how it came about.

There once was a shepherd who lived among the mountains with his wife and children; and so very poor was he that he often found it hard to give his family enough to satisfy their hunger. But he did not grumble; he only worked the harder; and his wife, though she had scarcely any furniture, and never a chance of a new dress, kept the house so clean, and the old clothes so well mended, that, all unknown to herself, she rose high in the favour of the all-seeing Frigga.

Now one day, when the shepherd had driven his few poor sheep up the mountain to pasture, a fine reindeer sprang from the rocks above him and began to leap upward along the steep slope. The shepherd snatched up his crossbow and pursued the animal, thinking to himself: "Now we shall have a better meal than we have had for many a long day."

Up and up leaped the reindeer, always just out of reach and at length disappeared behind a great boulder just as the shepherd, breathless and weary, reached the spot. No sign of the reindeer was to be seen, but, on looking round, the shepherd saw that he was among the snowy heights of the mountains, and almost at the top of a great glacier.

Presently, as he pursued his vain search for the animal, he saw to his amazement an open door, leading apparently into the heart of the glacier. He was a fearless man, and so, without hesitation, he passed boldly through the doorway and found himself standing in a marvellous cavern, lit up by blazing torches which gleamed upon rich jewels hanging from the roof and walls. And in the midst stood a woman, most fair to behold, clad in snow-white robes and surrounded by a group of lovely maidens.

The shepherd's boldness gave way at this awesome sight, and he sank to his knees before the Asa, Frigga, for she it was. But Frigga bade him be of good cheer, and said: "Choose now whatsoever you will to carry away with you as a remembrance of this place."

The shepherd's eyes wandered over the glittering jewels on the walls and roof, but they came back to a little bunch of blue flowers which Frigga held in her hand. They alone looked homelike to him; the rest were hard and cold; so he asked timidly that he might be given the little nosegay.

Then Frigga smiled kindly upon him.

"Most wise has been your choice," said she. "Take with the flowers this measure of seed and sow it in your field, and you shall grow flowers of your own. They shall bring prosperity to you and yours."

So the shepherd took the flowers and the seed, and scarcely had he done so when a mighty peal of thunder, followed by the shock of an earthquake, rent the cavern, and when he had collected his senses he found himself once more upon the mountain side.

When he reached home and had told his tale, his wife scolded him roundly for not bringing home a jewel which would have made them rich for ever. But when she would have thrown the flowers away he prevented her. Next day he sowed the seed in his field, and was surprised to find how far it went.

Very soon after this the field was thick with tiny green shoots; and though his wife reproached him for wasting good ground upon useless flowers, he watched and waited in hope until the field was blue with the starry flax blooms.

Then one night, when the flowers had withered and the seed was ripe, Frigga, in the disguise of an old woman, visited the lowly hut and showed the shepherd and his astonished wife how to use the flax stalks; how to spin them into thread, and how to weave the thread into linen.

It was not long before all the dwellers in that part of the earth had heard of the wonderful material, and were hurrying to the shepherd's hut to buy the bleached linen or the seed from which it was obtained. And so the shepherd and his family were soon among the richest people in the land; and the promise of Frigga was amply fulfilled.

CHAPTER IV

How a Giant Built a Fortress for the Asas

*This is the tale the Northmen tell of how
a giant once built a fortress for the Asas*

ALTHOUGH their city of Asgard was beautiful beyond compare, the Asas who lived therein could not forget that the race of the giants kept unwearying watch to do them despite. Even All-Father Odin was troubled when he remembered Mimir's warning that the draught of wisdom would ever work strife between the races of Asas and giants. And so at length the Asas, meeting in their Council Chamber at the roots of the Tree of Life, resolved that something more should be done to guard themselves. Already, it is true, the watchman Heimdall kept ward over the Rainbow Bridge by night and day, blowing a soft note on his horn to announce the coming or going of the Asas, but prepared to give a terrible blast should any of the Frost Giants attempt to cross the bridge.

Heimdall, however, might be overpowered before aid could reach him, and so it was decided to build, just within Asgard, a great fortress, which should be so strong that the Asas could rest safely behind its walls, even if the Frost Giants should invade their city.

The next question was, Who should build this fortress?

None of the Asas knew of a likely architect, and while they were discussing where one should be found, the horn of Heimdall rang out in token of the approach of a stranger.

Out rushed the Asas, and there, in parley with Heimdall, stood a gigantic figure with powerful limbs, on which the muscles stood out like ropes of iron.

Heimdall was speaking sharply, for he did not altogether like the stranger's look. "For what purpose do you come?" he was inquiring.

"I am a Master Builder," replied the stranger. "I can build towers and forts more strongly than any other builder in all the world. Have you anything of the kind that wants doing here?"

The eyes of the Asas met as they heard these words, and Odin, stepping forward, said, "Can you build us a fortress so strong that not all the strength of the Frost Giants could avail against it?"

"Ay, that can I," replied the stranger. "Look at my strong arms and see the breadth of my chest. If you will set me to work you shall soon find my worth as a Master Builder."

"How long will the fortress take to build?" asked Odin.

"I will build it for you in three half years," replied the stranger.

"And what do you ask as wages?" said Odin, and the Master Builder answered promptly:

"You must give me the sun, the moon, and Freya for my wife."

At these words the Asas, who had been pressing forward to hear the conference, fell back with muttered disapproval. For Freya was the most beautiful maiden in Asgard, the joy and pride of the city, ever young and ever fair; and the sun and moon were the light and life of men in the world below. So they bade the Master Builder come again next day, and meantime retired to their Council Hall to consider the matter.

All-Father Odin was for sending the Builder promptly about

his business when he returned for their decision, but his brother Loki counselled a different course.

Red Loki was a mischievous, sly fellow, full of wiles and deceit, and always quick to suggest a way out of a difficulty. On this occasion his plan was to allow the man to build the fortress, and to promise him the terms demanded, but subject to the condition that he fulfilled his task in a way that would be impossible for him fully to carry out.

His eloquence persuaded the Asas, and next day, when the Builder returned for their decision, Loki, as their spokesman, called to the mighty fellow as he crossed the bridge:

"Good man, we cannot wait for three half years for the completion of our fortress. But if you will undertake to do the work in the course of one winter, without any assistance, you shall have Freya, and the sun and moon to boot. If, however, on the first day of summer, one stone is missing from its place, the fortress will be ours without any payment whatever, since you will have broken your plighted word."

At this the Master Builder did not look well pleased. He pulled his great beard and eyed the speaker doubtfully, muttering that the time was too short for so great a task; but when Loki pretended to turn away, as though the matter were ended, he called after him:

"Well, have it so—the fortress shall be built in the time you set. But you must at least let me have the help of my good horse Svadilfare to carry stone."

When they heard this request the Asas demurred, saying: "He means to play us some trick."

But Loki persuaded them to make this trifling concession.

"For," said he, "of what use can a horse be in building a fortress? He will never be able to finish the place in time, and we shall get our fort for nothing. At least you can let him have his great clumsy horse for any use that he may be."

So the Asas agreed, and went their different ways, leaving the Master Builder to his work.

The winter months passed on, and while the Asas busied themselves with their various occupations and amusements, the

Master Builder was toiling with might and main. But he could have done little in the time if he had not had the help of his wonderful horse Svadilfare, who not only dragged huge blocks of stone to the spot, but raised them into position with his strong forefeet. And this was done with such speed that, some days before the end of winter, the fortress was finished, with the exception of three blocks of stone which were to form one of the gateways.

Then the Asas suddenly realised what was about to happen. In less than three days more the fortress would be finished; it needed, in fact, but one night's work to make all complete. They remembered with horror the price they had undertaken to pay; the loss not only of Freya, fairest of maidens, but also of sun and moon, whose light was the joy of their life and the necessity of mankind.

"It is Red Loki," said they, "who has brought us to this sad pass." So they began to reproach him very bitterly, threatening even to kill him if he did not find some way to evade the loss which threatened them.

At length, being really frightened, Loki promised to do something—anything, that would prevent the Master Builder from finishing the work during the three days that yet remained of winter.

That same night good Svadilfare was painfully dragging a great block of stone along the path to the new-built fortress, when Red Loki, changed into the semblance of a pretty little grey mare, came running up, saying, as plainly as horses can speak:

"Down below there is a delightful green meadow. Do come with me, and take a holiday from this ever-lasting work."

Scarcely had he heard her neigh when the steed kicked off his harness, left the block of stone to roll down the steep hill, and rushed after the mare. Away ran Loki, away ran Svadilfare, and after them rushed the Master Builder, shouting and yelling in vain. The noise they made was terrific, for the gallop of the horses and the *thud, thud,* of the mighty Builder shook the walls of Asgard and made the earth-dwellers shrink in terror from what they imagined to be thunderstorms and earthquakes. But the Builder never found his horse, for Loki had lured him to a meadow hidden safely away within a secret grove.

When the Master Builder returned to the fortress the first day of summer had dawned, and lo! the winter was gone, and the gateway of the building was unfinished.

Before it stood the Asas, and All-Father Odin greeted the Builder with:

"See, fellow, here is the first day of summer and your task is not yet fulfilled. Begone, then, from Asgard, for we are free from our bond, and would have no further dealing with thee or thy evil brood."

Then the Builder perceived that Odin knew who he really was, and with a roar of rage he returned to his own form, and stood revealed as a mighty Frost Giant, almost as huge as the fortress he had built.

Shaking his great fist at the Asas, he shouted threateningly:

"Ye have tricked and fooled me enough. Not for nothing does a Frost Giant stand within the walls of Asgard. Were it not so strongly built I would now tear down this fortress that I have raised; but your own palaces are not giant-built, and see to it that they are not soon tumbling about your ears!"

And in good sooth he might have torn down the very halls of the Asas in his rage, had not Thor at that moment dashed up the Rainbow Bridge in his chariot drawn by goats. For all this while Thor, the strongest of the Asas, had been away on a long journey; and had this not been so, the giants would have had little cause to fear.

Springing from his chariot as the furious giant was about to pull the roof off Valhalla, Thor gave him so mighty a blow on the head with his huge hammer that his skull broke into little bits and his body fell down into the Land of Mists.

"Take that for your wages," roared Thor, as he swung his hammer on high, "and in this same manner will I repay all of the race of Frost Giants who seek to set foot in Asgard."

And so in this way was built for the Asas a fortress so strong that none of the giant folk could dare to raise hand against it. But always it lacked three stones in the gateway, for no one except a Frost Giant could lift such mighty blocks into place.

CHAPTER V

The Magic Mead

This is the tale the Northmen tell of how All-Father Odin brought the Magic Mead to Asgard

THERE once lived among the earth-dwellers a certain man named Kvasir, who was very wise. He did not keep his wisdom to himself, as Mimir did, but went his way through all the world, answering questions and sharing his gift with those who cared for it. And wherever he went men were the better for his silver words, for Kvasir was a poet, the first who ever lived, and by his gift of poetry he made glad the hearts of gods and men.

Now when the dwarf people saw how Kvasir was loved and honoured, they grew jealous of him, and plotted to work him evil. So two of their number, called Fialar and Galar, met Kvasir one day and begged him to visit their cave under the earth and to take counsel with them concerning a very secret and important matter.

Glad, as was his wont, to help others, Kvasir agreed, whereupon the dwarfs conducted him into a dark and dismal place underground; and there, taking him unawares, they treacherously slew him, and poured his blood into three jars. This they mixed with honey, and thus made a Magic Mead, of such a nature that whoever drinks of it receives the gift of poesy, and his speech is silver and his heart is filled with wisdom.

It was not long before the gods in Asgard, missing the sweet sound of Kvasir's voice throughout the earth, began to make inquiries as to what had become of him.

The wicked dwarfs had spread the report that the wise man had choked by reason of his great wisdom. But All-Father Odin knew well that this absurd tale was not true, and was on the watch to see what mischief Fialar and Galar had been brewing.

Meantime, the dwarfs did not taste a drop of the Magic Mead, but hid it away in a secret place, while they went off in search of further adventures.

After awhile they found the Giant Gilling fast asleep by the seashore, and they began to pinch him till he was wide awake.

"Take us for a row on the sea, Gilling," they shouted, in their impudent little voices.

So the Giant Gilling, who was good-natured and stupid, got into a boat, and being very lazy, allowed the dwarfs to take the oars and row where they would.

Then Fialar and Galar rowed on to an unseen rock and upset the boat, so that the giant, who could not swim, was drowned; but they themselves perched astride on the keel, and the boat soon drifted ashore.

Hurrying to the giant's house they told his wife, with a fine pretence of sympathy, that her husband had fallen into the sea and was drowned. At this the poor giantess began to sob and groan until the walls shook with the noise. Then Fialar said to his brother:

"Tired am I of this bawling. I will now take her out, and as she passes through the doorway, drop a millstone on her head; and then there will be an end to them both."

Forthwith he asked if it would not comfort her to look upon the sea where her dear husband lay drowned; and she said it would. But as she passed through the doorway wicked Galar, who had scrambled up above the lintel, dropped a millstone on her head, and so she too fell an easy victim to the malice of the cruel brothers.

Now while the two dwarfs were jumping and skipping about in their wicked glee at the success of their evil plans, the Giant Suttung, son of Gilling, came home, and finding that his mother and father were both dead, he quickly guessed who were at the bottom of the mischief, and determined to put an end to the wretches.

Before they could evade his wrath, he grasped one of the dwarfs in each of his great hands, and, wading out into the ocean, he set them down upon a rock which he knew would be flooded at high tide, and there left them.

Then Fialar and Galar began to scream with terror, and to offer anything that Suttung chose to ask for, if only he would spare their lives.

Now Suttung had heard, as most people had done, of the Magic Mead, and he thought that this was a fine opportunity of getting it into his possession. So he bargained with the dwarfs, and they gladly promised to give him the whole brew if only he would save them from their perilous plight.

Suttung waited till they had had a good fright, and then, as the first wave washed over them, he waded to the rock and lifted them off. He took good care, however, not to give them their liberty until they had handed over the three jars of Magic Mead.

The moment he had got the precious jars into his possession Suttung hid them in a cave deep down in the centre of a mountain, and he set his daughter, Gunlod, the Giant-Maiden, to keep watch and ward, charging her to guard the cavern night and day, and to allow neither gods nor men to have so much as a sip of the marvellous liquid.

Meantime, All-Father Odin had sent forth his ravens, Hugin and Munin, to find out what had become of the wise Kvasir. For a while even they were puzzled by his complete disappearance, but presently they heard men talk of the Magic Mead that had been made from his blood, and so, little by little, they learned the truth, and flying back to Odin, they perched on his shoulders, and whispered it into his ears.

Now All-Father Odin was sorry for Kvasir, but he was still more vexed to think that this wonderful gift of poetry should be in the hands of his enemies, the giants. He began, therefore, to consider how he could get it from them, for though he had drained the draught of wisdom in speech and song, and nothing save a draught of the Magic Mead would bring him that gift.

So once more All-Father Odin disguised himself as an aged wanderer, pulled his grey hat well over his brows, threw his storm-hued cloak around him, and journeyed to the Land of Giants.

Searching about for the home of Suttung, Odin presently passed by a field where nine ugly serving-men were mowing hay. Now these were the servants of Baugi, the brother of Suttung, as Odin very well knew; so, after watching them for awhile, he called out:

"Hi, fellows! Your scythes are blunt. Would you like me to whet them for you?"

Glad of an excuse to stop work, the men shouted, "Yes."

Then Odin took a whetstone from his belt and whetted the scythes till they were sharp as razors.

The servants were much struck with the speed and skill with which this was done, and they all called out together to ask if the whetstone was for sale.

Odin replied that he was willing to sell it if he could get a fair price; upon which they all yelled at once that they would pay whatever he asked.

"Then let him have it who catches it," said Odin, and with that he threw the whetstone up in the air.

And then a tremendous struggle began. Each man fought with his neighbour for the stone and hacked at him with his keen scythe; and within a very few minutes all the nine serving-men lay dead on the field.

With a grim smile at the greed and quarrelsome behaviour which had brought them to this end, Odin passed on to the house of the Giant Baugi, and begged for supper and shelter for the night. The giant received him hospitably enough, and was about to sit down to table with him, when word was brought that his nine servants had killed each other and lay dead in the field.

Then Baugi began to complain and lament his bad luck, saying: "Here have I never had a better harvest, and yet there is not a man left to gather it in."

"Suppose you give *me* a trial," suggested Odin, "for though I look old I can do the work of nine men, and that you will soon find."

"What do you want for your wages?" asked Baugi doubtfully, for he guessed that the stranger was somebody out of the common.

"Nothing but a draught of the Magic Mead stored away by your brother Suttung," answered Odin calmly.

"'Tis no easy thing you ask of me, good fellow," replied Baugi, "nor is it mine to give. But if you will do my work I will go with you to my brother when all is done, and we will do our best to get the mead."

So Odin set to work all that summer-time, and never before had Baugi had such service done. Then, when the first breath of frost touched the autumn leaves, the toiler laid aside his tools and, going to his master, asked for his reward.

But Baugi shook his head doubtfully. "'Tis a harder matter than you think," said he. "Come with me, however, and I will do my best for you."

So they went together to the house of Suttung, and Baugi entered in and boldly asked his brother to give him a drink of the Magic Mead, wherewith to reward his servant.

At this Suttung flew into a great rage, and reproached Baugi for asking such a thing. "You have been fooled," he cried, "for this is none other than one of the gods, our deadly enemies, who, when he drinks the mead, will use his new-found wisdom in our despite. If you take my advice, you will do this enemy an ill turn while you have him in your power."

So Baugi went back to Odin, his heart torn between hatred of the god and fear as to what would happen if he did not keep his promise; but he only told gloomily that he had failed to get the mead.

Then Odin said, "If Suttung will not give the mead because of your promise, we must get it by some trick. And you will have to help me in this, because of your plighted word."

To this Baugi pretended to agree, but all the while he was trying to think of a plan whereby he could make an end of his troublesome servant.

They now made their way to the mountain where Gunlod kept watch over her treasured jars of mead. But her cave was hidden far away in the centre of the mountain, and none but Suttung knew how to find the entrance.

Baugi only pretended to join in the long and fruitless search, and at length, tired out, Odin took from his pocket an auger, wherewith holes are bored, and bade the giant use his great strength to drill a hole through the mountain to the cave.

Accordingly Baugi bored away and presently cried out, "See, there is your hole right into the cave!"

But Odin warily blew into the hole, and immediately chips of rock and dust flew back into his face, showing that the hole extended only a little way.

Then Odin knew, what before he had only guessed, that Baugi was trying to trick him; but he only looked at him grimly and said:

"Bore deeper, master, bore deeper."

And the giant was so frightened by the gleam in the iron-grey eye that he seized the auger, and this time made a hole which really pierced the mountain and penetrated to the hidden cave.

Directly Odin had made sure that Baugi had fulfilled his task, he changed himself into a snake and wriggled into the hole before Baugi had realised what had happened.

The next moment Baugi gave a stab at the snake with the sharp auger, hoping to cut him in two, but Odin was too quick for him, and he wriggled out of sight as the blow fell.

Odin crept a long way through the mountain until he came at length to a dark cave; and then he took again the form of the Father of Gods and Men.

Looking about him for awhile in the dimness of the cavern, he saw at length the beautiful Giant-Maiden, resting her head wearily on her hands and gazing at the great jars of mead which stood before her on a ledge as though she hated their very sight.

Coming softly to her side, Odin bent over her and gently kissed her forehead. Gunlod at this sprang up in terror, but when she saw Odin's kind face, her fears vanished and she smiled back at him.

"Whence come you?" asked the beautiful Giant-Maiden.

"I come from a long, long way off," replied the god, "and I am thirsty after my journey. May I taste the mead that stands in yon vessels?"

Gunlod shook her head till her long golden locks fell in confusion over her like a shower of laburnum blossom; but Odin set himself so winningly to coax her that, after she had held out for some long time, she told him at last that he might take one sip from each jar.

The words were hardly uttered ere Odin seized the first jar and in a moment had drained it dry. Then he snatched up the second and the third; and before Gunlod realised what had happened he had kissed her again, and, passing rapidly through the hole, had flown forth into the fresh air in the form of an eagle, and was bearing away the precious mead in his mouth to Asgard.

Meanwhile, Baugi had gone back to the Giant Suttung with the tale of how he had seen the mysterious serving-man change into a snake and wriggle through a hole in the mountain; and Suttung at once guessed that they had to deal with Odin himself. So he hurried to the hole and sat there to watch for the return of the snake.

But he had to wait so long that at length he grew drowsy, and in order to keep awake he was just pricking himself with the branch of a neighbouring thorn-bush, when *birr! whizz!* a great bird dashed out of the hold and made off into the upper air.

This awoke Suttung effectually. He knew he had missed a good chance of killing Odin, and that, in all probability, in the very act of carrying off the Magic Mead to Asgard; but he would not give up all hope, and next moment, in the form of another eagle, he was pursuing his enemy in eager flight.

Now Odin was heavy with the mead he had drunk, and his head was dizzy, so that he did not always fly along the straightest path. Little by little Suttung gained on him therefore, till it became very uncertain whether Odin could first reach the walls of Asgard.

The loud rush of fast-beating wings through the air attracted the attention of the gods, and they crowded to the walls of Asgard to watch the progress of the eagle, in whom they easily recognised Odin.

Some prepared great dishes in which to receive the Magic Mead from his mouth; others, seeing that he might be caught by his pursuer before he could reach the city, gathered a great pile of wood outside the walls, and heaped it with tow and tar and turpentine. To this they set fire, just as Odin flew over the battlements. And the flames shot up and burnt the wings of the pursuing eagle, so that Suttung tumbled to the earth and could fly no more.

Odin, exhausted and breathless, was meantime filling the dishes which the gods held ready for the Magic Mead, but so hurried was he that some of it was spilt a few scattered drops fell on to the earth below.

Men rushed eagerly to catch the precious drops in their mouths; but none could get enough to be made wise with the true spirit of poesy. Some caught enough to become makers of rhymes and verses, but this is a different thing.

The Magic Mead was henceforth kept in Asgard under the charge of white-haired Bragi, the son of Odin, he who plays so beautifully upon the harp that it seems to sing of itself.

And once or twice in every hundred years or so, the gods allow some very favoured babe of mortal man to drink a full draught of the Magic Mead. Then, when the child grows up, he becomes a great poet, and people say he is "inspired."

CHAPTER VI

How Loki Made a Wager with the Dwarfs

This is the tale the Northmen tell of how
Loki once made a Wager with the Dwarfs

A MOST mischievous and tricky god was Loki, always on the look-out to play some wicked prank which was sure to bring trouble upon himself or others. It was, indeed, a wonder that the other Asas put up with him so long in Asgard; but then, you see, he was Odin's brother.

One day, when Loki was looking about him for diversions, he saw asleep in the sunlight Sif, the beautiful wife of Thor the Thunderer.

Now Sif was noted among all the dwellers in Asgard for her glorious hair, which hung down to her heels and was like a thick web of golden silk. When she stood up it covered her like a cloak, and when she lay down it was like a golden coverlet; and Thor, her husband, thought it was the most beautiful thing in all the habitation of the gods.

Now mischievous Loki saw her sleeping under the gleaming mass of golden web, and he took a pair of sharp scissors and cut it all off close to her head, so that she looked quite bald and ugly.

When Thor came home and saw what had happened, he was wild with fury, and guessing at once who had done the deed, he stamped off to find Red Loki, vowing that he would break every bone in his body.

Then Loki, when he heard the thunder of Thor's tramp and saw the lightning flash from his angry eyes, was terrified, and attempted to change himself into another shape; but before he could do so the wrathful god had gripped him by the throat and was shaking the life out of him.

"Let me go!" gasped Loki. "Let me go, and I will bring new hair for Sif ere the daylight's gone."

"Go, then," roared Thor, "but mind, if you break your word you will have not only to reckon with *me*, but with Odin and Frey as well."

Then, giving Loki a last shake, he sent him flying over the battlements and down the Rainbow Bridge like a falling star.

Now Loki was terrified at the result of his trick, and dread of the punishment that Odin might have in store for him, when he returned with the hair, began to assail him. So he determined to take back with him two presents, one for his mighty brother, and one for Frey, the god of the Golden Sunshine.

Leaping on to the earth, he quickly made his way through a hillside into the depths of the mountains, never stopping till he had reached the dark and gloomy district of Dwarfland.

For a time Loki could see nothing, though he heard on every side the tapping hammers and heaving bellows of the Little Men.

Presently, however, he distinguished a tiny furnace with its burning flame, and saw by its light a little squat figure, who pulled off his peaked cap and asked the visitor what he wanted.

"I want you to make me three gifts," said Loki; "one for Odin, and one for Frey, and the third must be golden hair that will grow upon Sif's head."

Now the dwarfs were anxious to keep on good terms with the gods, who could protect them against the giants; and so, when they heard Loki's request, they readily agreed to make the three things. Accordingly, they set to work upon a pile of golden nuggets, and spun from them a mass of the finest gold thread, so smooth and soft that it looked like the loveliest hair. This they gave to Loki, telling him that directly it touched the head of Sif it would become as a natural growth.

"Now give me something for Odin," said Loki, well pleased.

So the dwarfs set to work again, and presently fashioned the spear called Gungnir, which, however badly it might be aimed, was always sure to go straight to its mark.

Loki gratefully took the spear, and there now only remained the gift for Frey.

The dwarfs thought awhile, and then set to work upon a ship which, when pressed together, would fold up and go into one's pocket, but which, when allowed to expand, would hold all the gods in Asgard and their horses, would sail through air as well as on water, and would always get a favourable wind directly it hoisted canvas.

Loki was immensely pleased with these gifts, and went away, declaring loudly that his dwarf friends were the cleverest smiths in all the world.

Now it so fell out that his words were heard by another dwarf, named Brock, who came and stood in his way and looked with scorn at the ship and the spear and the golden web which he carried in his hands.

"A clumsy lot of things you have there!" he jeered. "Why, my brother Sindri could make gifts that are far more wonderful than those."

"My head against yours that he could not!" said Loki, getting angry.

"Done!" chuckled Brock with a leer, and forthwith they made their way to the underground cave where Sindri was at work in his forge.

Now Sindri was quite ready to take up the challenge, but only on condition that Brock would blow the bellows for him. Loki now began to feel uneasy, for he had hoped the dwarf would decline to compete when he heard what were the gifts he had to improve upon. But Sindri only wagged his long beard at them contemptuously, and Loki's head began to tremble for the result of his wager.

So he determined to try and hinder the work.

Meantime Sindri had thrown a pigskin into the furnace, and had gone outside to find a magic charm, saying as he went:

"Blow, brother, blow with all thy might till I return, and stay not thy hand for an instant."

Directly Loki heard this he changed himself into a great stinging fly, and lighting on Brock's hand, he stung him with all his might. But the dwarf never stopped blowing, though he stamped and roared with pain. Then Sindri returned, and going to the furnace drew from it a golden boar of great size, which had the power of flying through the sky and scattering light from his golden bristles as he flew. But Brock did not know all this, and looked somewhat scornfully at the gift, saying:

"I thought you could do better than this."

"Wait a bit," said Sindri, and with that he threw a lump of gold upon the fire and went out, charging his brother not to stop blowing for an instant.

Then in flew Loki again, still disguised as a gadfly, and lighted on Brock's neck and stung him so that the blood flowed. But though the dwarf yelled with pain he did not cease blowing.

When Sindri returned he pulled out of the fire a fine gold ring. And this ring was made in such a marvellous fashion that every ninth night nine other rings would drop from it, so that its owner would be the richest being in the world.

But Brock did not know all this, and only growled.

"Wait a bit," said Sindri again, and this time he threw a lump of iron on the fire, once more going out, and urging his brother, as he went, to be specially careful this time, or he would spoil all.

Then in flew Loki and lighted between Brock's eyelids, stinging them so that the blood poured down and blinded him. Raising his hand for a second the dwarf dashed away the blood, and just for that instant he ceased to blow. Presently Sindri was back again, saying gloomily that what lay in the furnace came nigh to being spoilt. Then he put in his hand and pulled out a great hammer; but the handle of the hammer was an inch too short.

Now this hammer was so powerful that no one, not even a Frost Giant, could resist its force, and it would smash a mountain as easily as it would an egg-shell. So Brock, when he knew all that was to be known, took the three gifts and hastened away to Asgard to pit them against those of Loki, who had just returned.

Enthroned in a circle sat the Asas, and in the midst, as judges of the gifts, sat Odin, Thor and Frey.

Loki of the red beard and cunning eye, bringing forward the magic spear, bowed low to Odin, saying: "Here, brother Odin, is a spear that will never miss its mark!"

Then he turned to Frey and handed him the magic ship, saying: "Here is a ship which will never lack a fair wind wherever you wish to go; and though you may fold it up and carry it in your pocket, it will hold all the gods of Asgard and their steeds besides."

But to Thor he gave the golden web of hair, and said nothing, for he feared him.

Then Brock stood forth and produced his treasures, saying: "Here, mighty Odin, is a ring that will produce nine other gold rings every ninth night."

Odin laughed with joy, and said: "Spears have I in abundance, but with this ring I shall never want for gold."

Next Brock opened the heavy bag with which his shoulders were burdened, and out of it fell the golden boar, which he laid before Frey, saying: "Here, good Frey, is a boar who will carry you through the air or over the sea. And wherever you go on his back the sky will be lighted up by his golden bristles."

Then Frey laughed with joy, saying: "Better sport is it to ride on a golden boar than in a ship."

Lastly Brock drew out the short-handled hammer named Miölnir. And this he gave to Thor, saying: "Most powerful one, here is a hammer whose blows nothing can withstand, not even mountains or Frost Giants; and however far you throw it, this hammer will always return to your hand."

Then Thor jumped from his seat joyfully crying out: "Better than the golden hair of Sif is a weapon against which none of my enemies can stand. Brothers, let us decide this wager forthwith. And for me, I give my vote in favour of the gifts of Brock."

Then the gods and goddesses put their heads together and came to the conclusion that the hammer of Thor was worth all the gifts of Loki twice over; for with it they could be protected against the Frost Giants, who were always their secret dread. So they decided:

"Brock has won the wager. Let Loki lose his head."

Much dismayed, Red Loki offered to pay a huge ransom, but of this Brock would not hear.

Then Loki pretended to give in. "Come and take me then," he cried, but when the dwarf tried to seize him he was already far away, for he wore the shoes with which he could run through the air and over the sea.

And knowing that he could never catch him, Brock was beside himself with rage. Looking round him he saw that, though the others had dispersed, Thor was still playing with his new hammer, smashing a mountain here and a great tree there.

"Mighty Thor," cried the dwarf, "will you do something for me in return for my gift? Bring to me that fellow who has broken his word, that I may slay him forthwith."

With a nod of his great head Thor jumped into his goat chariot, and was soon thundering through the air after wicked Loki. Driving with the speed of lightning he quickly overtook the fugitive, whose plea for help, however, touched him so that he relented and bethought him of a way in which he might save his life.

Justice must be done, however, so he dragged the culprit back to Asgard and gave him over to Brock; but he warned the dwarf that although the head of Loki was rightfully his, he must not touch his neck.

Now Brock could not possibly cut off the one without touching the other, so he bethought him of another plan. He would at any rate sew up the bragging lips that had caused so much trouble and told so many lies since All Things began.

So he took a strong piece of string and bored holes with his auger, and firmly stitched up the lips of Red Loki, and broke off the thread at the end of the sewing.

For a time after this there was peace in Asgard, and this would have lasted for long had not Loki managed at length to cut the string, when he became as talkative as ever.

And this is the end of the tale of How Loki made a Wager with the Dwarfs.

CHAPTER VII

The Apples of Youth

This is the tale which the Northmen tell of how the Apples of Youth were once very nearly lost to Asgard

SWEETEST of all the Asa folk was Idun, the fair young goddess of Springtime and Youth, and dearly loved was she by the other Asas, both for herself and for her magic apples.

Fast locked in a golden casket were her apples, ripe and sweet and rosy. And each day, at dawn, Idun came to the table where the gods sat and feasted together, and gave those who wished a taste of the fruit.

And it came to pass that everyone who ate the magic fruit grew fresh and young again, however old and weary he had been before. For even the gods of Asgard grew old and weary sometimes; and then nothing would make them young again but the Apples of Youth.

So Idun treasured the fruit with the greatest care, and never let it out of her charge for a moment. And however many she took out of her casket wherewith to feed the gods, there always remained just the same number as before.

> "Bright Iduna, maid immortal!
> Standing at Valhalla's portal,
> In her casket has rich store
> Of rare apples, gilded o'er;
> Those rare apples, not of earth,
> To ageing Asas gave new birth."

It was only to be expected, of course, that the fame of this magic fruit should spread, and as nobody liked to grow old, many of the giants, as well as the little dwarf people, used to come to the gates of Asgard and beg that Idun would give them a taste of her apples. But this, though they offered her the richest gifts they could think of, she never would do.

Now one day it so fell out that Odin grew weary of watching his heroes feast and fight in Valhalla, and determined to go forth and seek an adventure elsewhere.

So he called for his brother Hœnir, the clear-eyed Asa who first gave hope to the heart of man, and Loki, the mischievous fellow who yet by reason of his fun and gaiety was no bad travelling companion, and bade them accompany him on a journey.

Speeding over the Rainbow Bridge they came down to the world below, and presently found themselves in a desolate region of mountain and moorland, through which they wandered for a long, long time, without coming across any kind of human habitation.

At length, grown weary and very hungry, they began to look about for food, and presently saw, to their great joy, a herd of oxen feeding upon the mountain side. It took no long time to kill a fine bull and to kindle an immense fire; after which the Asas hung up the animal to roast and sat down to wait till it was done.

But though the fire flamed bravely over the logs, it made no difference whatever to the meat, which remained raw and cold.

Heaping on fresh fuel, the three Asas put the carcass still nearer the flame and waited hungrily. All in vain, the meat remained uneatable.

Looking at each other in dismay, the Asas exclaimed:

"There is some magic spell at work here."

And at that very moment they heard the loud croak of a bird in the tree above them.

Hastily searching the branches, the Asas soon found an immense eagle perched there and looking down upon them with an evil expression.

"Ho!" cried Odin, "is it you who has bewitched our food?"

The eagle nodded and croaked maliciously again.

"Then come at once and remove the spell," cried the famished Hœnir.

"If I do so, will you give me as much as I want to eat?" asked the eagle.

At this Odin hesitated, for he feared a trick, but Loki's mouth was watering, and he called out:

"Yes, yes, anything you like if you will only let the meat be cooked."

Then the great bird swooped down and began to fan the flame with his huge wings, and behold! in a very few minutes the gravy began to run, a delicious smell of roast beef filled the air, and there was the meat done to a turn.

Just as the three Asas were putting out hungry hands to seize their portions, however, the eagle, which had been hovering overhead, swooped down and seized more than three-quarters of the animal, leaving barely enough for one of the famished gods.

This was too much for Loki. With a roar of rage like that of an angry lion, he seized a great stake that stood near and struck with all his might at the greedy bird.

The eagle shook himself after the blow, but instead of dropping his booty he rose slowly into the air. And then, to Loki's dismay, he found that one end of the pole had stuck fast to the body of the bird, the other to his own hands.

Try as he would he could not let go, and so found himself being dragged along over stones and bushes and briers, while his arms were almost torn out of their sockets.

In vain he begged and implored the eagle to let him go; it took no notice of him whatever, but flew on and on, just a little way above the earth, until at length Loki, feeling that he could endure no longer, promised to give him anything he asked if he would only release him.

Then at last the eagle spoke, telling him that he would set him free on one condition only, and that was that he should manage, by some trick, to tempt Idun out of Asgard, in order that he could obtain possession of her and of the magic fruit. He told Loki, moreover, that he was the Storm Giant Thiassi in disguise, and bade him beware of the consequences if he broke his solemn promise to one of giant race.

By this time Loki was ready to promise anything to save his life, and so at length he found himself free.

Bruised and torn he made his way back to Odin and Hœnir, by whom he was closely questioned concerning his adventures.

But Loki never hesitated to depart from the truth, and, knowing that it would not do to tell what he had promised, he answered glibly that the eagle had captured him in mistake for someone else, and that when he found out it was Red Loki himself, he had set him free, with many expressions of sorrow for his error.

So the three Asas returned to Asgard, and from that moment Loki did not cease to plot and plan the means by which he could entice Idun outside the gates.

And indeed this was no easy matter, for the Apples of Youth were so precious to the gods that Idun was well guarded by night and day. Sometimes, however, even the Asas were off their guard, and that was the opportunity for Loki.

Strolling one day through the groves of Asgard, Loki found the beautiful maiden all alone in a sunny corner playing at ball with her golden fruit.

"Aha!" cried he, approaching gently so as not to startle her, "what a fair game thou playest here, maiden!"

But Idun only smiled at him happily and went on tossing her apples.

Then Loki pulled a long face, and came nearer, and said:

"Till this day, fair Idun, I had said that nowhere in the wide world grew apples like thine. But now have I found a tree whereon the fruit is of finer gold, and of greater size than these, and a taste of it needs not to be renewed again, but makes one young for evermore."

Then Idun stopped playing and her blue eyes grew dark and stormy, for she could not bear to think that her apples would no longer be the joy and delight of the Asas.

But then she remembered Loki's deceitful ways, and said: "I believe thee not. This is one of thy tricks, Red Loki."

"Ho, you think so, do you?" said the crafty one. "Then come and see them for yourself, and bring your own to compare with them."

"Are they near by?" said Idun, rising doubtfully to her feet, and still holding fast to the casket of fruit.

"Only just a little way off," replied Loki, and taking hold of her hand he drew her outside the thicket.

On and on they went, and when she asked where they were going he always replied that the grove where the apples grew was just a little farther than he had thought.

At length, without noticing that she had passed the boundaries, Idun stood outside the walls of Asgard on a dreary region of barren heath, and then she at last began to suspect mischief.

"Where am I?" she cried, "and where, O Loki, are the golden apples?"

But she only heard the jeering ha! ha! ha! of the Asa as he returned to Asgard, and that was soon lost in the *whirr-r-r* of wings as a mighty eagle, swooping down upon her, fixed his talons in her girdle and rose with her into the air.

And this, of course, was Thiassi, the Storm Giant, who had been on the watch for her all the time, and who now carried her off, casket and all, to the bleak and desolate abode over which he ruled. Well had it been said that Loki was at the bottom of all the misfortunes that ever befell in Asgard. And never until the End of All Things would he work so dire a mischief again.

Poor Idun grew pale and thin and sad in her captivity, but she would not purchase freedom with a taste of the Apples of Youth, although the Storm Giant coaxed and begged and threatened by turns.

For a time the Asas took little notice of her absence, for they thought she was amusing herself somewhere in the sunny groves of Asgard and had forgotten her daily visit. Then they began to feel old and weary, and at first scarcely knew what was wrong.

Glancing at each other they saw, with startled eyes, wrinkles and lines and grey hairs where these things were not wont to be. Their youth and beauty were disappearing, and then they suddenly awoke to the need of a thorough search for the missing Idun.

And, when she could nowhere be found, All-Father Odin, mindful of former tricks, sent for Red Loki and began very closely to question him. Others had seen Idun in his company on that eventful day when she had been carried away, and so, finding it impossible to keep the matter hidden, Loki confessed, with a mocking laugh, that he had betrayed her into the power of the Storm Giant.

Then all the Asas arose in hot wrath and threatened Loki with death or torture if he did not at once restore the beautiful Goddess of Youth with her magic fruit. And at length, being fairly frightened, he undertook to bring her back, if Freya would lend him her falcon plumes that he might disguise himself as a bird.

Thus equipped, Loki flew off to Giantland, and arrived, fortunately for him, just as Thiassi had gone out a-fishing.

High up at the window of a great stone castle fair Idun looked with tearful eyes upon the stormy sea, and, as she thought of the sunny groves of Asgard, suddenly the plumage of a great falcon almost brushed against her face. Drawing back in alarm, she saw the cunning red eyes of Loki looking at her from the bird's head.

"See how kind am I!" he jeered. "I am come to take thee back to Asgard."

Then Idun almost wept for joy, till she remembered that she was a prisoner, and so cried pitifully:

"I cannot win forth from this cold stone tower, O Loki, and even if I could, thou canst never carry me and my casket back to

Asgard. And lo! I cannot outrun the wicked Storm Giant, and though the fruit be heavy, I will not leave it behind."

Then Loki soothed her, and by his magic arts he changed her into a nut, which he took up in one talon, while the casket he carried with the other, and so set off to fly back to Asgard.

Now Thiassi, the Storm Giant, was ill at ease that day, for he felt the pangs and pains of old age upon him as he went a-fishing. So he determined to return earlier than usual, in order to try once more to get the magic fruit from Idun.

Judge then of his dismay when he found his prisoner flown!

Hastily transforming himself into an eagle, Thiassi began to scour the regions of the air, looking everywhere for the maiden, and before long he noted the steady flight of a falcon towards the walls of Asgard.

Sweeping towards him through the air, the keen eyes of the eagle saw the gleam of a golden casket in his talons, and he knew that it was an Asa who had come to the rescue of Idun.

And now it seemed that Loki would be hard put to it to reach Asgard before he was overtaken; for the eagle swept through the air with his great wings much faster than the falcon could fly, and the Asas, who had assembled on the battlements of the city to watch the race, trembled for its issue.

Then some of them remembered how once before they had played a trick upon the pursuer in a similar conflict, and they collected pine shavings in great abundance and piled them on the walls, and stood ready to fire them when the moment came.

On, on flew Loki, hard beset; and close behind him came, with steady rush, the mighty eagle Thiassi. He was almost upon his prey as they neared the walls, but Loki made a last violent effort, which was successful, and he fell exhausted into the midst of the Asas.

At the same moment the pile of fuel was lighted, and Thiassi, blinded with smoke and singed with flame, dropped over the battlements, and thus fell an easy prey to his waiting enemies. In admiration of his good race, however, the Asas placed his eyes as stars in the heavens, and there they shine to this day.

So the Apples of Youth returned to Asgard, and all the Asas hastened to eat of them and became young and beautiful again.

And fair Idun once more resumed her shape, and never again was tricked by wicked Loki, but played with her magic fruit in the golden groves of Asgard till the End of All Things.

And this is how the Apples of Youth were once very nearly lost to Asgard.

CHAPTER VIII

How the Fenris Wolf was Chained

*This is the tale the Northmen tell of
how the Fenris Wolf was chained*

FAIR as were the meads of Asgard, we have seen that the Asa folk were fond of wandering far afield in other regions. Most restless of all was Red Loki, that cunning fellow who was always bringing trouble upon himself or upon his kindred. And because he loved evil, he would often betake himself to the gloomy halls of Giantland and mingle with the wicked folk of that region.

Now one day he met a hideous giantess named Angur-Boda. This creature had a heart of ice, and because he loved ugliness and evil she had a great attraction for him, and in the end he married her, and they lived together in a horrible cave in Giantland.

Three children were born to Loki and Angur-Boda in this dread abode, and they were even more terrible in appearance than their mother. The first was an immense wolf called Fenris, with a huge mouth filled with long white teeth, which he was constantly gnashing together.

The second was a wicked-looking serpent with a fiery-tongue lolling from its mouth.

The third was a hideous giantess, partly blue and partly flesh-colour, whose name was Hela.

No sooner were these three terrible children born than all the wise men of the earth began to foretell the misery they would bring upon the Asa folk.

In vain did Loki try to keep them hidden within the cave

wherein their mother dwelt. They soon grew so immense in size that no dwelling would contain them, and all the world began to talk of their frightful appearance.

It was not long, of course, before All-Father Odin, from his high seat in Asgard, heard of the children of Loki. So he sent for some of the Asas, and said:

"Much evil will come upon us, O my children, from this giant brood, if we defend not ourselves against them. For their mother will teach them wickedness, and still more quickly will they learn the cunning wiles of their father. Fetch me them here, therefore, that I may deal with them forthwith."

So, after somewhat of a struggle, the Asas captured the three giant-children and brought them before Odin's judgment-seat.

Then Odin looked first at Hela, and when he saw her gloomy eyes, full of misery and despair, he was sorry, and dealt kindly with her, saying: "Thou art the bringer of Pain to man, and Asgard is no place for such as thou. But I will make thee ruler of the Mist Home, and there shalt thou rule over that unlighted world, the Region of the Dead."

Forthwith he sent her away over rough roads to the cold, dark region of the North called the Mist Home. And there did Hela rule over a grim crew, for all those who had done wickedness in the world above were imprisoned by her in those gloomy regions. To her came also all those who had died, not on the battlefield, but of old age or disease. And though these were treated kindly enough, theirs was a joyless life in comparison with that of the dead warriors who were feasting and fighting in the halls of Valhalla, under the kindly rule of All-Father Odin.

Having thus disposed of Hela, Odin next turned his attention to the serpent. And when he saw his evil tongue and cunning, wicked eyes, he said:

"Thou art he who bringest Sin into the world of men; therefore the ocean shall be thy home for ever."

Then he threw that horrid serpent into the deep sea which surrounds all lands, and there the creature grew so fast that when he stretched himself one day he encircled all the earth, and held his own tail fast in his mouth. And sometimes he grew angry to think that he, the son of a god, had thus been cast out; and at those times he would writhe with his huge body and lash his tail till the sea spouted up to the sky. And when that happened the men of the North said that a great tempest was raging. But it was only the Serpent-son of Loki writhing in his wrath.

Then Odin turned to the third child. And behold! the Fenris Wolf was so appalling to look upon that Odin feared to cast him forth, and he decided to endeavour to tame him by kindness so that he should not wish them ill.

But when he bade them carry food to the Fenris Wolf, not one of the Asas would do so, for they feared a snap from his great jaws. Only the brave Tyr had courage enough to feed him, and the wolf ate so much and so fast that the business took him all his time. Meantime, too, the Fenris grew so rapidly, and became so fierce, that the gods were compelled to take counsel and consider how they should get rid of him. They remembered that it would make their peaceful halls unholy if they were to slay him, and so they resolved instead to bind him fast, that he should be unable to do them harm.

So those of the Asa folk who were clever smiths set to work and made a very strong, thick chain; and when it was finished they carried it out to the yard where the wolf dwelt, and said to him, as though in jest:

"Here is a fine proof of thy boasted strength, O Fenris. Let us bind this about thee, that we may see if thou canst break it asunder."

Then the wolf gave a great grin with his wide jaws, and came and stood still that they might bind the chain about him; for he knew what he could do. And it came to pass that directly they had fastened the chain, and had slipped aside from him, the great beast gave himself a shake, and the chain fell about him in little bits.

At this the Asas were much annoyed, but they tried not to show it, and praised him for his strength.

Then they set to work again upon a chain much stronger than the last, and brought it to the Fenris Wolf, saying:

"Great will be thy renown, O Fenris, if thou canst break this chain as thou didst the last."

But the wolf looked at them askance, for the chain they brought was very much thicker than the one he had already broken. He reflected, however, that since that time he himself had grown stronger and bigger, and moreover, that one must risk something in order to win renown.

So he let them put the chain upon him, and when the Asas said that all was ready, he gave a good shake and stretched himself a few times, and again the fetters lay in fragments on the ground.

Then the gods began to fear that they would never hold the wolf in bonds; and it was All-Father Odin who persuaded them to make one more attempt.

So they sent a messenger to Dwarfland bidding him ask the Little Men to make a chain which nothing could possibly destroy.

Setting at once to work, the clever little smiths soon fashioned a slender silken rope, and gave it to the messenger, saying that no strength could break it, and that the more it was strained the stronger it would become.

It was made of the most mysterious things—the sound of a cat's footsteps, the roots of a mountain, the sinews of a bear, the breath of fishes, and other such strange materials, which only the dwarfs knew how to use.

With this chain the messenger hastened back over the Rainbow Bridge to Asgard.

By this time the Fenris Wolf had grown too big for his yard, so he lived on a rocky island in the middle of the lake that lies in the midst of Asgard. And here the Asas now betook themselves with their chain, and began to play their part with wily words.

"See," they cried, "O Fenris! Here is a cord so soft and thin that none would think of it binding such strength as thine."

And they laughed great laughs, and handed it to one another, and tried its strength by pulling at it with all their might, but it did not break.

Then they came nearer and used more wiles, saying:

"*We* cannot break the cord, though 'tis stronger than it looks, but thou, O mighty one, will be able to snap it in a moment."

But the wolf tossed his head in scorn, and said:

"Small renown would there be to me, O Asa folk, if I were to break yon slender string. Save, therefore, your breath, and leave me now alone."

"Aha!" cried the Asas. "Thou fearest the might of the silken cord, thou false one, and that is why thou wilt not let us bind thee!"

"Not I," said the Fenris Wolf, growing rather suspicious, "but if it is made with craft and guile it shall never come near my feet."

"But," said the Asas, "thou wilt surely be able to break this silken cord with ease, since thou hast already broken the great iron fetters."

To this the wolf made no answer, pretending not to hear.

"Come!" said the Asas again, "why shouldst thou fear? For even if thou couldst not break the cord we would immediately let thee free again. To refuse is a coward's piece of work."

Then the wolf gnashed his teeth at them in anger, and said:

"Well I know you Asas! For if you bind me so fast that I cannot get loose you will skulk away, and it will be long before I get any help from you; and therefore am I loth to let this band be laid upon me."

But still the Asas continued to persuade him and to twit him with cowardice, until at length the Fenris Wolf said, with a sullen growl:

"Have it your own way then. But, as a pledge that this is done without deceit, let one of you lay his hand in my mouth while you are binding me, and afterwards while I try to break the bonds."

Then the Asa folk looked at one another in dismay, for they knew very well what this would mean.

And while they consulted together the wolf stood gnashing his teeth at them with a horrid grin.

At length Tyr the Brave hesitated no longer. Boldly he stalked up to the wolf and thrust his arm into his enormous mouth, bidding the Asas bind fast the beast. Scarce had they done so when the wolf began to strain and pull, but the more he did so the tighter and stiffer the rope became.

The gods shouted and laughed with glee when they saw how all his efforts were in vain. But Tyr did not join in their mirth, for the wolf in his rage snapped his great teeth together and bit off his hand at the wrist.

Now when the Asas discovered that the animal was fast bound, they took the chain which was fixed to the rope and drew it through a huge rock, and fastened this rock deep down in the earth, so that it could never be moved. And this they fastened to another great rock which was driven still deeper into the ground.

When the Fenris Wolf found that he had been thus secured he opened his mouth terribly wide, and twisted himself right and left, and tried his best to bite the Asa folk. He uttered, moreover, such terrible howls that at length the gods could bear it no longer. So they took a sword and thrust it into his mouth, so that the hilt rested on his lower, and the point against his upper jaw. And there he was doomed to remain until the end of All Things shall come, when he

> "Freed from the Chain
> Shall range the Earth."

CHAPTER IX

How the Pride of Thor was Brought low

*This is the tale the Northmen tell of how the
Pride of Thor was once brought low*

FROM the sunny heights of Asgard the Asa folk were wont to look upon the earth and to take pleasure in its welfare and in the happiness of its people. But all too often they saw with dismay that the Frost Giants from their cold Northern home of ice and snow sent forth cruel blasts which nipped the buds, withered the flowers of spring, and saddened the hearts of men. So, one day, that mighty Asa who is called Thor determined to go forth and teach these Giant folk how to behave themselves better. Calling for his chariot of brass, which was drawn by two mighty goats, from whose teeth and hoofs sparks continually flew, he was about to drive away, when Red Loki came running up and begged to be taken too.

To this Thor agreed, for he had rather a liking for Loki, in spite of his mischievous tricks, and in a few minutes they were hurtling through the air at a great rate.

All day long they drove, and at evening time reached the

borders of Giantland, where stood the hut of a poor peasant. Seeing this, the two Asas determined to try to obtain shelter for the night.

The peasant was a good-hearted fellow, and gladly welcomed them under his roof; but he had only a bit of black bread to offer them for supper, and this was by no means a satisfactory meal for two hungry gods.

But Thor was quite equal to the occasion.

"Fear not," said he kindly, "I will provide meat in plenty for you and your family as well as for ourselves."

Then he went out, killed his two goats, cut them up and threw them into a great cauldron, which the peasant's wife, at his request, had set to boil upon the fire. The skins, meantime, he spread with care upon the floor.

The stew was soon cooked to perfection, whereupon Thor invited the man and his wife and children to eat as much as they would.

"Be careful, however," said he, "not to break a single bone, but to throw them all into the skins spread out on the floor."

This they promised to do, but during the meal Red Loki, wishing to see what would happen if they disobeyed, persuaded the boy, Thialfi, the peasant's son, to break one of the bones in order to suck out the marrow, saying that no one could possibly know that he had done so. Then they lay down to sleep, the bones of the animals wrapped in the goat skins being upon the floor.

Next morning, just before daybreak, Thor arose, and, having stretched himself, took up his mighty hammer and gave the goat skins a tap. Immediately the goats sprang up, as much alive as ever they were, and perfectly well, save that one of them limped.

Then Thor knew at once that his commands had been disobeyed, and the whole household soon knew it too. His brows sank over his eyes, and he grasped his hammer so hard that his knuckles grew white. The terrified peasant fell down on his face before him; and when Thor lifted the hammer to destroy him the whole household wept aloud and begged for mercy, promising to give him all they had in the world as an atonement.

When Thor saw their terror, his anger left him, and he agreed to take as a ransom the children of the peasant, a boy and girl, called Thialfi and Roskva. And they became his servants, and have been always in his company since that time.

Leaving his goats in charge of the peasant, Thor went forward towards Giantland, accompanied by Loki and the two children; and the boy Thialfi, who was the fleetest of foot of all living creatures, carried Thor's bag.

After walking all day through a bleak and barren country wrapped in a thick mist, they came at nightfall to a great wood, which seemed to offer neither provisions, nor roof to shelter under for the night.

At length, after searching about for a very long time, they came to what seemed to be a large hall of misty and uncertain shape, the door of which was as wide as the whole building.

So they entered, and, finding everything within empty and dark, they determined to go no farther, and stretched themselves, hungry and weary as they were, upon the ground.

In the middle of the night they were awakened by what seemed to be a great earthquake. The earth trembled beneath them and the house shook.

Calling upon his companions, Thor arose, and fearing lest the roof should fall upon them he drew them into an inner room and, seating himself in the doorway, took up his hammer and prepared to defend himself and them, if anything should befall. But nothing further happened save a renewed trembling of the ground and a curious, regularly recurring sound, like a loud groan or roar.

When it began to grow light Thor went out and saw, not far off, a huge giant lying on the ground fast asleep; and he understood that it was his snores which had caused the ground to shake and which had sounded like a roar or groan.

Suddenly the giant awoke and sprang up, so quickly that Loki and the children, who had followed Thor, jumped behind a tree. But Thor, who was afraid of nothing, only grasped his hammer tightly and asked his name.

"I am called Skrymir," said the giant, looking down at him, and, catching sight of his hammer, of which all in heaven and earth had heard, he went on: "I don't need to ask *your* name, for I see you are Thor. But what have you done with my glove?"

As he said these last words, he stretched out a huge hand and picked up his glove, which Thor, to his great astonishment, found to be the house in which he had spent the night; and the inner room was the place for the thumb.

Hearing that they were on their way towards Giantland, Skrymir asked if he might accompany them; and as he seemed a good-natured fellow they agreed. But first they sat down to eat their breakfast.

Skrymir ate his huge meal out of a great provision sack, and eyed with much merriment the wallet which held the food of Thor and his companions.

"'Tis like a little toy," said he; but Thialfi answered crossly:

"Toy it may be to you, but it has made my shoulders ache very finely, I can tell you. I could hardly sleep all night for the pain."

Then Skrymir laughed, and took the bag and put it into his sack, slinging the whole over his shoulder as if it had been a feather-weight.

After this they all set off together, and that day they covered an immense distance, for the giant took such huge strides that they had to run the whole time in order to keep up with him.

When it grew dark, Skrymir led them into a vast wood where no habitation was to be found, and bade them take up their quarters under a huge oak. The others were weary and hungry beyond words, for they had not stopped all day either to eat or rest; but Skrymir seemed only sleepy, and was preparing to begin his snores when Loki, whom fasting had put decidedly out of temper, sharply reminded him that they had had no supper. Pushing the great sack over to them, the giant sleepily replied that they were welcome to all that it contained, and immediately fell into a deep slumber.

But when Loki tried to undo the mouth of the sack he could not get one knot loosened, nor could he even get one of the strings to stir. Then Thor tried with all his strength, but could do nothing. This was a serious matter, for they were all starving with hunger by this time; so Thor, in a great rage, snatched up his hammer in both hands, stepped up to where Skrymir was lying and dashed the hammer, with all his force, at his head.

At this blow, which would have smashed the skull of most men, the giant drowsily opened one eye, saying: "Did a leaf fall on my head just now? Good-night to all of you. I suppose you have now had your supper and are going to bed."

At this the Asas were so astonished that they meekly replied that they were just going to do that very thing. And they went and lay down under another oak. But there was no sleep for them, for, besides their fear and hunger, the whole wood resounded with the giant's snores, so that it seemed as though it thundered all the time.

At last Thor could stand it no longer, so he went over to him, and swinging his hammer with all his skill brought it down with such a crash that he knew by the feel of it that it had sunk deep into the head.

But the giant only turned over, saying sleepily: "What was that? Did an acorn fall upon my head? How is it with you, friend Thor?"

Then Thor answered hastily that he had only just waked up, and that it was midnight and still time to sleep.

The god was now alarmed, and he decided that, if it were possible, he would get in a third blow which should put an end altogether to the most extraordinary companion he had ever had.

So he lay watching for Skrymir to go fast asleep again, and shortly before daybreak his chance came.

Creeping up, he clutched the hammer with all his might and dashed it at the giant's temples with such force that it sank up to the handle.

Scarcely had he time to pull it out again than Skrymir sat up and began to yawn, rubbing his eyes and stroking his temples and saying:

"Are there any birds sitting in the tree above me? I thought, as I woke up, that some moss from the branches fell upon my head. Ho, there! Thor, are you awake? You seem to be moving early this morning. Let us all get up and continue our journey, for we are now not far from Giant Town."

Filled with astonished dismay at the failure of his attempts, Thor roused his companions, and all set off, hungry and dispirited, at the giant's heels. Presently they began to whisper together as to the events of the night, and of the enormous strength and size of their companion, but after awhile Skrymir looked down at them and said:

"We have now come to two ways; mine goes to the north where you see yon mountains; yours, if you still wish to reach Giant Town, lies there to the east. So here we part company, but first let me give you some useful advice.

"I have heard you whispering to one another that I am not small of stature; but when you come to Giant Town you will see greater folk still. So do not brag too much of your own powers, for the Giant folk will not put up with the boasting of such insignificant little fellows as you be.

"But if you want to be quite wise, turn back now to your own place, for that is the best thing you can do."

So saying, Skrymir shouldered his great sack and, turning his back upon them, went off through the forest with such huge strides that he was soon lost to sight.

Now Loki was much disposed to follow the advice of the giant and turn back to Asgard, but of this Thor would not hear. So they continued their journey until noonday, when they saw before them a great town standing in the midst of an immense plain. The walls and gates of the town were so high that they had to bend their necks right back before they could see to the top of them, and when they came nearer still they found the gate was fast shut.

But this gate had bars, and was made to keep in the Giant folk, not to keep out smaller people, of whose visits they had never thought. So the two Asas and their servants found little difficulty in creeping through the bars, and so getting into the town.

The first thing they saw was a great hall, towards which they went, and finding the door open they entered, and saw in the centre of it two benches, enormously high and wide, upon which sat a number of giants. In their midst, upon a platform high as the roof of an ordinary house, sat the King of the Giants, to whom they advanced and made their bows. At first the King looked about on the floor as though they were too small for him to see, but at length he cast a scornful glance upon them, and with a grin that showed all his teeth, said:

"Is this little fellow the great god Thor, of whom we have heard so much? Perhaps, however, you are bigger in strength than in size. Now, for what feats are you and your companions prepared? For you must know this, that no one is allowed to stay here unless he be more skilled in some craft or accomplishment than any other man."

At this Red Loki, who was so dreadfully hungry that he scarcely knew what he was saying, called out: "I know what I can do better than anyone else! I will soon prove that there is no one present who can eat his food faster than I can."

Then said the King of the Giants: "That is a feat to be proud of, if you speak the truth, and you shall try it immediately."

So he called from the bench a man called Logi, and bade him come out on the floor and try his strength against Loki.

The others took a huge trough full of meat and set it on the floor, and they put Logi at one end and Loki at the other.

Both of them ate as fast as they possibly could, and met in the middle of the trough. But though Loki had such an immense appetite, and had eaten every scrap of meat off the bones, Logi had eaten up the flesh and the bones and the trough as well.

So Loki had to confess that he had been beaten.

Then the Giant-King looked at the boy Thialfi and asked: "What use is that lad in heaven or earth?"

And Thialfi answered that the would run faster than anyone whom the Giant-King liked to name.

"That is a good feat," said the King, "but it is to be hoped you can run *really* fast, for you will have something to do to win this race."

So saying he took them outside, where there was an excellent racecourse along the flat plain; and he called up a young man, whose name was Hugi, and bade him run a race with Thialfi.

In the first heat of that race, although Hugi ran so fast, yet, when he turned to run back, he met Thialfi face to face. Then the King of the Giants encouraged the lad, saying: "Never before has come anyone hither who was swifter of foot than you."

Then they ran the second heat, and when Hugi reached the goal, Thialfi was three quarters of the way thither.

Then said the giant: "Well run, Thialfi; yet I do not think that you will win this race. However, we shall see what happens in the third heat."

When this was run, Hugi had reached the goal and turned back again ere poor Thialfi was barely half way there.

At this all the giants began to applaud Hugi, saying that he had fairly won the race; and Thialfi was obliged to go sadly away.

The King of the Giants next inquired what feats Thor could show to prove the truth of the tales men told of his great strength; and the Asa, who was now very thirsty, and at all times a mighty man at the bowl, said that he would drink deeper than anyone in the whole world.

So they returned to the hall, where the King called upon his cup-bearer to bring the horn out of which his valiant giants drank; and this was filled with ale and handed to Thor.

Then said the King of the Giants: "With us 'tis thought that the man is a good drinker who empties this horn at one draught; he who takes it off in two is but moderately thirsty; but he who cannot empty it in three is but a wretched drinker, and not worthy of the name."

Thor looked at the horn, and thinking within himself: "This is not a difficult task, for the horn, though it seems deep, is not very large," took a drink which he quite thought would have drained the vessel. But when he could drink no longer, for lack of breath, he looked in the horn, and there was the ale still brimming over the edge.

Then the giant chuckled and said: "Well drunk, good Thor, but you have by no means emptied the horn. It seems to me, indeed, that men have boasted too much of your fine deeds. I would not have believed that you would have taken so long to drink up the ale. However, I don't doubt you will finish it at the second draught."

Thor reddened with wrath at these scoffing words, and took up the horn, intending to drink the ale to the last dregs. But, try as he would, he could not get the end of the horn to tip up completely, and when he set it down it seemed to him that he had drunk less than at the first time. Yet some difference had been made, for the horn could now be carried without spilling.

"Ha! ha!" laughed the giant. "Is this your skill, good Thor? Are you not leaving rather much for your third draught? It looks to me as if that will have to be the greatest of them all."

Then Thor got very angry indeed, and, setting the horn to his mouth, drank with all his might and main, so that when he could do no more and had set it down again, the ale had certainly grown less.

"Ha! ha!" roared the giant. "They think too highly of you in the world above, my little Thor. Now what other game would you like to try?"

"Whatever you like," answered Thor very grumpily, for none of the Asas liked being laughed at.

So the giant said: "Young lads here think it nothing but play to lift my cat up from the ground, and I should never have suggested such a feat to the strength of Asa Thor had I not discovered that he is much less of a man than I thought."

Then he called: "Puss! Puss!" in a voice that shook the house; upon which an enormous grey cat sprang forth on the floor before them.

Rather annoyed at being asked to do such an easy thing, Thor went over to the animal, put his arm round it and tried to lift it up. But the more he tugged and strained the more the cat arched its back, so that his strength was exerted vainly; and in the end, when he was black in the face with the efforts he had made, he had only succeeded in lifting up one paw.

Then the giant repeated his scornful laugh, saying: "That's just as I expected. The cat is rather large, and Thor is small—tiny, indeed, compared with the great men who are here with us."

"Tiny, indeed!" roared Thor, in great wrath. "Let anyone you like come and wrestle with me and I will show you if my strength is as tiny as you seem to think."

At this giant pretended to look about him on the benches, saying: "I don't see anyone here who would not think it beneath him to wrestle with such a puny fellow. Let me see! Let me see! Ah! call hither my old nurse, Elli, and let Thor wrestle with her if he wants to. She has thrown to the ground before now men who thought themselves as strong as this little Thor."

At his call there came into the hall an old woman—so old that Thor refused at first to close with her. But the giants mocked him so that at length he seized her round the waist. Yet the tighter he grasped her the firmer she stood. At length she began to grip him in her turn. Thor lost his footing almost at once and, though he wrestled valiantly, she brought him on to his knee.

At this the giant interfered, saying that no more was necessary to show who was the stronger, and that it was getting too late for any more such contests. Then he bade them seat themselves at supper, and after a royal feast conducted them to their beds with the kindest hospitality. But Thor spent all that night in bitterness, for his pride had been brought very low.

At daybreak next morning the Asas and their companions arose and prepared to depart. Before they set out, however, their host appeared on the scene and insisted upon their eating a hearty breakfast, after which he offered to show them the most direct way out of the city.

As they set out, the Giant-King grew strangely silent and thoughtful and did not speak to them until they stood outside the gates. Then as they were about to bid him farewell, he suddenly asked Thor how he thought his journey had turned out.

To this Thor, deeply humbled and mortified by all that had occurred, said that he felt much disgraced at the knowledge that henceforth the giants would call him a man of little account. But to his intense surprise the giant shook his head, saying: "Had I my way, you should never enter this city again, and if I had known before how strong you were, you should never have come into it, for you have very nearly brought utter ruin upon us all.

"Know then, first of all, that I have deceived you with magical delusions the whole time. For I was that giant Skrymir who met you in the woods, and who tied up the mouth of the provision sack with invisible iron threads, so that you could not unloose it.

"That same night you struck with your hammer three great blows upon my head, the least of which would have made an end of me if it had hit me. But in the darkness I managed each time to bring a mountain between me and your hammer without your seeing it; and if you want to see the marks you made in it you have but to look at that mountain above my city, with its top cloven into three great dales.

"Next, when you came to my hall, Loki contested with Logi, my courtier, as to who should eat the fastest. But he whose name was Logi is really *Fire*, and in consequence he could eat up trough and bones and all in no time. When Thialfi ran his race, he ran against Hugi, who is no other than *Thought,* and no one, of course, can run as fast as he.

"When you yourself drank from that horn, then indeed was seen a marvel which I should never have thought possible. You did not see that one end of the horn stood in the sea, which you were drinking all the time. And when you reach the shore you will see how much the sea has ebbed by your draughts.

"Nor was it less marvellous to me that you lifted up the paw of the cat. For that cat was none other than the Serpent which lies around the whole earth with its tail in its mouth. When it took the form of a cat you lifted it so that it was obliged to arch itself almost up to the sky; and then we all trembled, for we feared that you would pull it altogether out of the sea.

"Your struggle with Elli was perhaps the most amazing of all. For she is *Old Age,* of whom none has ever got the better.

"And now depart, O Asa folk, and 'twill be better for us both if we never see each other again."

Now when Thor heard how he had been tricked, he grasped his hammer with intent to dash both the giant and his city in pieces. But when he looked for them, both had disappeared, and he found himself standing with his companions in the midst of a large plain, on which was no sign of habitation.

Then he knew that the power of the Giant folk would not yield to force, and thinking of their strange adventures Thor and his companions returned to Asgard.

Chapter X

How Thor's Hammer was Lost and Found

This is the tale the Northmen tell of how
Thor's Hammer was lost and found

M OST precious in the eyes of Thor was his magic hammer, Miölnir, of which even the mighty Frost Giants stood in dread.

Always he laid it by his side when he went to rest, and always it was the first thing for which his hand was outstretched when he awoke. Judge then of his horror and dismay when, on opening his eyes one morning, the hammer was nowhere to be seen.

Starting up with a roar of rage, Thor commenced to search everywhere for the missing weapon. Up and down his wonderful palace, built of the thunder clouds, he tramped, with a noise that shook the whole city of Asgard. But the hammer was not to be found.

Then he called upon golden-haired Sif, his wife, and bade her help in the search; and still the hammer was nowhere to be seen. It was clear that someone must have stolen it, and, when he realised this, Thor's wrath broke all bounds. His bristling red hair and beard stood up on end, and from them flew a whole volley of fiery sparks.

Presently, as the angry Asa was shaking the palace with his thunderous voice, Red Loki came along to inquire into the trouble. He was not likely to sympathise with Thor, but, always brimful of curiosity, he loved to have a part in everything that happened.

"What's the matter, Asa Thor?" said he; and Thor replied, lowering his voice as he spoke, for he did not want his loss to be too widely known:

"Now listen to what I tell thee, Loki—'tis a thing which is known neither on earth below nor in heaven above. My hammer's gone."

This news was most interesting to Loki, who had long owed Thor a grudge, which he was afraid to pay openly. "Ho, ho!" said he. "Then shall we soon have the giants turning us out of Asgard, brother Thor."

"Not if you use your wits as you know how," growled Thor, still in a very bad temper. "Come, you call yourself a clever fellow. Find out for me who has robbed me of my thunderbolt, my hammer, my Miölnir."

Then Loki gave a grin and a wink, and promised to do what he could—not because he cared for Thor, but because he loved to be of importance, and was, moreover, really frightened as to what might happen to Asgard if the magic hammer was not at hand.

It was not long before he noticed that an extraordinary kind of tempest was raging in the regions below—not an orderly kind

of tempest, with first some thunder, and then some rain, and
then a gust of wind or two, such as Thor was wont to arrange,
but a mixture of hail and wind and thunder and lightning and
rain and snow, all raging together in a tremendous muddle, so
that the earth folk thought the end of the world was come.

This gave Loki a hint, and he began to peer about between
the clouds, until at length he saw that the trouble was coming
from a certain hill which stood in the centre of Giantland.

Now on the top of this hill lived a certain Thrym, prince of the
Frost Giants, who for a long time past had been very envious of
the might of Thor. He had, indeed, done his best to imitate him
as far as he could, and had managed to get up a very good imi-
tation of lightning and hail and rain; but he had not been able to
manage the thunderbolts, for they could only be made by means
of Thor's hammer, Miölnir.

All this was well known to Red Loki, and he was therefore not
at all surprised to find that, somehow or other, Thrym must have
got hold of the magic weapon; for here were thunderbolts crash-
ing about the earth and sky at a terrible rate.

When informed of the discovery, Thor flew into a still more
tremendous rage, and wanted to rush off at once to try conclusions with the giant. But Loki, who loved rather to get a thing
by trickery and deceit, persuaded him that violence would
never do.

"Remember," said he, "that Thrym *with* the hammer is much
stronger than Thor without it. This is a matter which must be
managed by clever wit and craft, not by force and loud talking.
Leave therefore the whole matter to me."

To this Thor very reluctantly agreed.

Then Loki bethought him of some disguise wherein he might
visit Giantland in safety, for he was not at all anxious to risk his
life. He betook himself to the House of Maidens, over which
ruled Freya, fairest of all in Asgard, she who was wont to shake
the spring flowers from her golden locks as she passed over the
frozen uplands, leaving behind her a region of green and smiling beauty. Loki found the goddess, and begged the loan of her
magic falcon plumes, in which she was wont to flit to and fro
over the earth; and when she learnt for what purpose he needed
them she gladly assented.

Then Loki took the appearance of a great brown bird, and spreading his wings he flew away towards Giantland.

It was a long journey, as he already knew, and, although the tempest had now ceased to rage, he found the country of the giants darker and colder and drearier than ever.

The longest journey comes to an end, and at length Loki reached a mountain where sat the Giant Thrym, his huge legs dangling to the ground, playing with a puppy as large as an elephant.

Perching as near as he dared, Loki gazed at the giant with his bright, round eyes, and was wondering how to begin, when Thrym, who, at a glance, had seen completely through his disguise, said calmly, in a voice as much as possible like Thor's thunderous roar: "Oh, ho! Loki, what are you doing so far from Asgard? Are you not afraid, little fellow as you are, to venture alone into our country?"

Then Loki, thinking to win his way by flattery, replied: "Sad indeed is it in Asgard, now that Miölnir has vanished. Clever was that one who spirited it away from the very side of Thor. Methinks none but you could have done it, O mighty Thrym!"

Pleased with the compliment to his cleverness the giant chuckled before admitting: "Ay, Loki, the hammer is mine, 'tis very true; and now men will know who really is the Thunderer."

"Ah well!" sighed cunning Loki, "some men are strong by reason of their weapons, and some are just as strong without. Small need have you, O mighty Thrym, for hammers, but Thor is naught without it. Yet, since all the world knows that you are his master, let him have his plaything back, that we may cease to be troubled by his peevish outcry."

But though Thrym was as stupid as he was big, he was not to be caught thus.

"No, no, my little Loki," he said. "Mine is the hammer, and deep have I buried it beneath the bottom of the sea. Go, tell this to your Asa folk, and say to them that I will give it back on one condition only—and that is, that they send me Freya, that fairest of maidens, to be my wife."

At this suggestion Loki could scarcely keep from laughing, for the idea of sending the beautiful Freya, the joy and delight of Asgard, to be the wife of this ill-favoured Frost Giant was too absurd for words.

It was not much to him, however, what happened to anyone except himself, so he hastened to reply: "Be sure, O Thrym, that everything I can do to further the matter shall be done. And if Freya is of the same mind as I you will soon be welcoming that most sweet maiden to Giantland—farewell!"

So saying, he spread his brown wings and flew back to Asgard, delighted to think of the mischief he could now set brewing.

First of all he visited Thor, and told him of what had passed. And the Thunderer, when he heard of Thrym's boastful words, was filled with wild wrath and wanted to start off, then and there, and wrest the hammer from the depths of the sea. But Loki pointed out the difficulties that stood in the way and, leaving the Asa to ponder over his words, he hurried off to Freya and informed her of Thrym's proposal.

The beautiful Freya was walking in her garden, and round her neck she wore her famous necklet of stars. When she heard Loki's suggestion that she should wed a hideous giant she fell into such a rage that she broke her necklace, and all the stars went falling through the sky, so that men cried: "See how the stars are shooting!"

Meantime the Asa folk had met together to consider all that had happened, and, having calmed the fury of Thor, they pointed out to him that Asgard stood in the gravest danger of an attack which would find them quite unprotected. When they had said this several times over, Thor began to weary of the subject, and he replied with great surliness: "Very well, then. Let Freya go to Thrym as his wife, and then shall we be as before, with Miölnir to defend us."

When Freya heard this, her rage turned to tears and lamentations, and she declared that it would be death to her to send her to the gloomy halls of Giantland, whence she could never hope to revisit the flowery meads and grassy slopes of Asgard. And the Asas, unable to bear the sight of her grief, with one voice declared that they would never spare her from the Home of Bliss.

Then there stepped forward Heimdall, the watchman who sits on guard over the Rainbow Bridge by night and day.

Now Heimdall had the gift of seeing into the future, and the Asas were always ready to hear his words, well knowing them to be wise.

"My plan is this," said he. "Let Thor borrow the clothes of Freya and put a thick veil over his face; and let him go thus to Thrym's castle and pass for his bride. And if he cannot by some means manage to get hold of the hammer when he is there— why, he must give it up altogether."

At this suggestion the Asas clapped their hands with approval—all, indeed, save Thor, who looked most glum, and was extremely unwilling to agree to the plan.

"Dress me as a bride!" he grumbled. "A pretty maiden I shall make. Ready enough am I to fight, but I will not make myself a laughing-stock if I know it."

But the Asas besought him to give way, while Loki twitted him with cowardice. Fair Freya, too, appealed with tearful eyes; and so at length, with great reluctance, the Thunderer agreed to do what they wished.

Fortunately the maiden Freya was very tall, but even so it was with some difficulty that they managed to cover the burly form of Thor with her robes.

He insisted, moreover, upon wearing his own shirt of mail and his girdle of strength; and these took much drapery to hide. Great was the laughter in the halls of Asgard that night as the Battle Maidens brushed and curled Thor's long yellow hair, and set a jewelled headdress upon it; and finally, when the maidens proceeded to cover up his thick beard and angry eyes with a silken veil, the mirth of the Asas was unrestrained. To complete the disguise, the maidens hung round his neck the famous necklet, which had now been re-strung, and finally Frigga, the wife of All-Father Odin, secured at his girdle the great bunch of keys proper to brides at a wedding in the Northland.

While this was being done, Loki, more than all, had been convulsed with merriment at the success of his mischief-making. The very sight of Thor's disgusted looks, and of his great hands clenched with rage under the delicate veil, nearly killed him with laughter; and when all was ready he declared himself unable to lose an atom of the fun in store.

"Let me go with you," he implored. "See, I will dress myself as your handmaiden. Ah, you had better agree, for without me to prompt you, you will never play your part."

So Loki was dressed as a waiting-maid, and took his seat very demurely by the side of Thor in the goat-car. Loud was the laughter in Asgard as the Asas watched the two drive off together and heard the roar of the Thunderer's voice issuing from the folds of a meek maiden's veil as he urged his goats upon their course. Long and stormy was that ride to Giantland, for Thor was still in the worst of tempers, and drove his chariot so furiously that

> "The mountains crashed,
> The earth stood in flames,"

as the hoofs of the goats clattered over mountains and waters, striking sparks wherever they touched a rock.

Thrym was much overjoyed when he heard that a chariot containing the two maidens was approaching his door. Away ran his servants in different directions, some with orders to make ready a grand banquet, some to prepare the chamber of the bride, some to receive her at the door.

The giant himself assisted them to alight, and looked with admiration at the stately figure of his bride; but he made no attempt to see her face, since it is the custom in the Northland for the bride to remain veiled until the marriage has been completed.

"A bride worthy of a giant!" murmured his servants, as he led her to a lofty seat beside his own great throne of gold; and they looked with approval also on the buxom form of the waiting-maid, who stood, closely veiled, behind her mistress' chair.

Now the journey had been long and cold, and it was with joy that the new-comers noticed that the preparations for the banquet were complete, for they were exceedingly hungry.

The giants are huge eaters, and they gathered round the board, whereon were displayed an enormous ox roasted whole, a vast dish of salmon and various other dainties. But because the bride was a woman, and modest withal, they brought her tiny morsels on a dainty golden plate.

This was too much for Thor, who had always possessed a most healthy appetite, and was now more than usually ready for his supper. Gradually drawing nearer to the table, whilst the others were busy with the meal, he managed to get hold of the dish of roasted ox, and within a few minutes the whole of the animal had disappeared.

Then he put out his hand to the platter of salmon, and in eight mouthfuls disposed of eight of the great fish. After this he noticed a large plate full of cakes and sweetmeats, which was set apart for the ladies of the party. Of these, too, he made short work. Finally, feeling thirsty after his huge meal, he took up two barrels of mead, and tossed them off, one after another, down his capacious throat. Then he sat back on his chair with a sigh of deep content.

These proceedings had been watched by Loki with uneasiness, but by Thrym with open-mouthed dismay. Was this the usual appetite of this dainty maiden, who had eaten more than the company of giants? But Loki bent towards him and whispered in his ear that the thought of marrying had so excited Freya that she had eaten nothing for eight days, and had therefore been on the point of starvation.

This reassured the giant, and being now himself filled with mead he drew nearer and, lifting a corner of the veil, tried to kiss the cheek of his future bride.

But Thor, who was longing to be at close grips with him, threw him such a fiery glance that he drew quickly back, saying: "Why does fair Freya's eye burn like a spark from a furnace?" "Pooh!" whispered Loki again, "that is nothing but her love for you, which for eight days has raged like a flaming fire."

This news was still more pleasant to hear, and Thrym, in high good humour, cried: "Bring in the hammer, my wedding gift, wherewith to plight the maid. For when I have laid it on her lap she will be my own for ever, and together we will work dire evil against the Asa folk, whom I hate with all my heart."

What was that unmaidenly sound that issued from under the silken veil at these words? But though Loki turned pale to hear it, Thrym, busy sending for the hammer, did not pay any heed.

Back came the giant's servants at length, bending under the weight of Miölnir. And as they bowed before the silent maiden, sitting with meekly bent head upon the throne, Thyrm cried with a merry jest: "See, here is little Thor's tiny plaything—a pretty toy truly for his feeble hands. Take it, fair Freya, as my wedding gift."

"And take *that* as mine!" roared Thor, in a voice of thunder, as he flung off the veil and rose to his full height. And with the words he swung the hammer once—and ere the eye could follow its movement, it had crashed through Thrym's skull, and had knocked over a round dozen of his guests. Yet again did it swing in the Asa's hand, and this time it left not a giant standing in the hall.

A third time it was swung, and on this occasion the roof and walls of the palace came tumbling on every side, and only Thor and Loki were left alive amid the ruins.

"Ha! ha!" laughed Red Loki, "that was neatly done, fair Freya."

Thor, who was now busily tearing off the hated robes and veil, stayed to look threateningly at his companion. "No more of that, Loki," said he, "the thing had to be done, 'tis true, but talk not to me again of this woman's work. We will remember only that I am the Thunderer, and that my hammer that was lost is found."

So they drove back peacefully to Asgard.

And this is the end of the tale of How Thor's Hammer was lost and found.

CHAPTER XI

The Giant's Daughters

This is the tale the Northmen tell of how the Giant's Daughters tried to kill Thor

UGLIEST and wickedest of all the giants was Geirrod, who lived in a great gloomy castle away in a dark corner of Giantland, with his two giant daughters, Gialp and Greip.

Hideous, indeed, were they, for, besides being of huge misshapen figure and clumsy of feature, the one had red eyes and the other had perfectly black teeth.

Now, when Geirrod heard of the death of Thrym, his brother, he waxed very wroth, and swore with a great oath that he would never rest till he had wreaked vengeance on Thor.

Loudly he described the terrible things he would do to him if only he could catch him without his hammer, his belt of power, and his gloves of might; and one ugly daughter blinked her red eyes, and the other gnashed her black teeth, and both clamoured to have what might be left of the Asa when their father had finished with him.

Meantime Thor was not even aware of the existence of these folk, and it did not seem at all likely that he would put himself in their way.

About the time that Geirrod was thus breathing out threats against the Thunderer, Loki grew restless within the walls of Asgard, and, recalling the fun he had had when he visited Giantland in the guise of a bird, he went to Freya once more with intent to borrow her falcon dress. But Freya would not lend it again, for she had no liking for Red Loki. So the mischievous fellow waited for a moment when she was busy watering the blades of young corn, and stole the dress.

Only a few moments passed ere Loki was on the wing. To and fro he flitted for awhile, and then directed his flight towards Giantland, until at length, as luck would have it, he found himself hovering above the towers of Geirrod's castle.

The giant and his family were sitting at their great table as Loki arrived upon the scene. Peering through the open window he could see the ugly trio snatching at the joints from the smoking dishes, and half choking themselves in their efforts each to eat faster than the rest.

Perching on the window-sill, Loki could not resist a croaking chuckle of amusement, and at the same time his great wings shut out much of the light, so that the giant's attention was attracted, and he looked quickly up.

"Ho! Catch me yon bird!" he cried to one of his servants, for there was that about the appearance of the falcon that revealed the truth to Geirrod at a glance.

The servant leapt at once to the window-sill; but the ledge was too high for him, and Loki croaked and chuckled at his vain attempts, keeping all but within reach in order to increase the fun.

But suddenly the servant, giving an extra high spring, managed to get a grip of the sill, and as Loki spread his wings in flight he found his feet firmly caught in some ivy. In vain he struggled to get free, the servant seized him fast and carried him off in triumph to Geirrod.

"Who are you?" asked the giant; but Loki only blinked and made no reply.

"What are you doing here?" he demanded again; but still he got only a blink for answer.

"Who sent you to spy upon us?" roared Geirrod; Loki gave only another blink.

Then the giant arose in wrath, and, declaring that hunger and thirst were the best things in the world to teach a bird to talk, he locked the unfortunate Asa in a strong cage, with neither food nor drink.

For three whole months he languished, and then at last, being at the point of death, he croaked out feebly that he was Asa Loki, and promised anything in his power if Geirrod would only set him free.

This was the chance which the giant had been waiting for.

"Bring me here," said he, "yon Thor of whom I hear so much, and see that he comes without his hammer or his belt of strength or his gloves of might."

And this Loki promised to do.

As soon as he was able, Loki flew back to Asgard, with a fine story composed upon the way. He told Thor that during his three months' absence he had been a welcome guest at the hall of a friendly giant, Geirrod by name; and that, when he had reluctantly torn himself away, the giant had expressed the strongest wish that he would revisit him, along with Thor the Thunderer, of whose brave deeds he had often heard tell.

Flattered by these honeyed words, Thor readily fell into the trap and agreed to accompany Loki to Geirrod's hall. He even laid aside his hammer, girdle, and gloves, when Loki pointed out that to wear such things would not be courteous to their friendly host.

Then the two set forth together.

Now on their way they passed the house of Grid, a kindly old giantess, who had long been a friend of Thor's. Sitting in her doorway, she saw them pass by, and beckoned to Thor to come to her, while Loki, unsuspecting, went on his way.

"Whence goest thou, Asa Thor?" asked the old giantess.

"To Geirrod's hall, good mother," he cheerfully replied. "Do you know him?"

"Know him!" said Grid, with a hoarse chuckle. "Is there anyone who does not know Geirrod? But why, my son Thor, do you go unarmed to the hall of the strongest and wickedest of all the giants?"

Then Thor ground his teeth, exclaiming: "This is another trick of that rascal Loki! And now, what is to be done, for if I return to fetch Miölnir, and my girdle of strength and my gloves of might, they will say that Thor is afraid."

Now Grid was possessed of a girdle of strength, a staff of power, and gloves of might, and these she produced and gave to Thor, bidding him say not a word about them.

And when Thor had thanked her he resumed his way after Loki.

Presently the two Asas came to the brink of a river which is the largest in all the world, and the waves were dashing far above their heads. Then Thor buckled on the belt of strength and, taking the staff firmly in his grasp, he stepped boldly into the water, while Loki clung to his belt, for he was afraid. Higher and higher rose the waves, and if Thor had not kept a firm grip on the staff of power he must have been washed away. But Loki, overcome with fear, let go of the belt and was carried by the waves back whence he came; and from thence he hastened back to Asgard as fast as he could run.

When Thor had reached midstream he saw Gialp, the red-eyed daughter of the giant, stirring up the water at its source with intent to overwhelm him. So, stooping quickly, he took up out of the river an enormous rock and threw it at her. He was not wont to miss his mark, and the giantess fled, howling. At once the waters abated, and Thor, seeing a mountain ash overhanging the river caught at it and pulled himself safely ashore.

This is why the mountain ash from that time has been called "Thor's Salvation."

Wearied with his journey, Thor gladly turned his steps towards Geirrod's hall, which loomed out of the darkness near by. He was received with much honour by the giant's servants, though Geirrod himself had not yet returned home.

A banquet had been prepared within the hall, and thither

Thor was conducted. But, somewhat to his surprise, he could see only one chair. This, however, was large and roomy, draped round the legs and comfortably cushioned, so the Asa was glad to throw his tired limbs upon it.

But scarcely had he done so, when the chair began to rise beneath him, and it ascended towards the rafters with such force and speed that in another moment Thor would have been crushed to death, had he not retained his hold of the staff of power. This he now pushed against the rafters, and at the same time he pressed down on the seat with such force that he descended again with a loud crash, which was mingled with shrieks and screams. For Gialp and Greip, the giant's daughters, had hidden themselves under the chair, intending to kill Thor, and had now met the fate which they had prepared for him.

After this, Thor proceeded to eat a good supper, and scarcely had he finished when the Giant Geirrod came striding into the hall.

He gnashed his teeth horribly when he saw Thor sitting quite at home, but he pretended that he was pleased at his visit, and at once invited him into another hall, where a number of large fires were burning.

Here he proceeded to challenge Thor to a contest of skill in throwing. The Thunderer, nothing loth, bade Geirrod give the signal.

But Geirrod, thinking to catch Thor off his guard, snatched up a red-hot wedge of iron from the fire and flung it at him.

Quick as lightning, Thor caught the wedge in his glove of might, and so forcibly did he throw it back that it passed through the giant, through the pillar in front of which he stood, through the wall of his castle, and at last buried itself fathoms deep in the rock without.

Nor was this all, for at the touch of the red-hot iron the body of Geirrod was turned into stone; this Thor now took and set up on top of a high mountain in Giantland; and it was long before any of the folk of that country dared try conclusions with the Thunderer again.

And this is the end of the tale of How the Giant's Daughters tried to kill Thor.

Chapter XII

The Story of Balder the Beautiful

*This is the tale the Northmen tell of the
sad fate of Balder the Beautiful*

Fair beyond all the sons of Odin was Balder the Beautiful, Balder of the snow-white brow and golden locks, and he was well beloved not only by the Asa folk, but also by the men of the earth below.

> "Of all the twelve round Odin's throne,
> Balder, the Beautiful, alone,
> The Sun-god, good and pure and bright,
> Was loved by all, as all love light."

Balder had a twin-brother named Hoder, who was born blind. Gloomy and silent was he, but none the less he loved his bright sun-brother best of all in heaven or earth.

The home of Balder was a palace with silver roof and pillars of gold, and nothing unclean or impure was allowed to come inside its doors.

Very wise in all magic charms was this radiant young god; and for all others save himself he could read the future; but "to keep his own life safe and see the sun" was not granted to him.

Now there came a time when Balder's bright face grew sad and downcast; and when his father Odin and his mother Frigga perceived this they implored him to tell them the cause of his grief. Then Balder told them that he had been troubled by strange dreams; and, since in those days men believed that dreams were sent as a warning of what was about to happen, he had gone heavily since these visions had come to him.

First he had dreamt that a dark cloud had arisen which came before the sun and shut out all brightness from the land.

The next night he dreamt again that Asgard lay in darkness, and that her bright flowers and radiant trees were withered and lifeless, and that the Asa folk, dull and withered also, were sorrowing as though from some great calamity.

The third night he dreamt yet again that Asgard was dark and lifeless and that from out of the gloom one sad voice cried:

"Woe! Woe! Woe! For Balder the Beautiful is dead—is dead!"

Odin listened to the recital of this story with heavy heart, and at its conclusion he mounted his coal-black horse and rode over many a hard and toilsome road till he came to the dark abode of Hela. And there he saw, to his surprise, that a great banquet was being prepared in the gloomy hall. Dishes of gold were set upon the table and all the couches were covered with the richest silken tapestry, as though some honoured guest were expected. But a throne that stood at the head of the table was empty.

Very thoughtfully Odin rode on through those dim halls till he came to one where dwelt an ancient prophetess, whose voice no man had heard for many a long year.

Silent he stood before her, until she asked in a voice that sounded as though it came from far away: "Who art thou, and from whence dost thou come to trouble my long rest?"

Now Odin was fearful that she would not answer him did he give his real name, so he told her that he was the son of Valtam, and asked anxiously for whom the grim goddess of death was preparing her banquet.

Then, to his great grief, the hollow voice of the prophetess replied that Balder was the expected guest, and that he would shortly be sent thither, slain by the hand of Hoder, the blind god of darkness.

"Who then," asked Odin, in sorrowful tones, "shall avenge the death of Balder?"

And she answered that the son of the Earth-goddess, Vali by name, should neither

> "Comb his raven hair
> Nor wash his visage in the stream,
> Nor see the sun's departing beam,
> Till he on Hoder's corse shall smile
> Flaming on the funeral pile."

And learning thus of the fate of his two favourite sons, All-Father Odin went sadly back to Asgard.

Meantime Mother Frigga had not been idle. Filled with anxiety for her darling son, she decided to send her servants throughout the earth, bidding them exact a promise from all things—not only living creatures, but plants, stones, and metals, fire, water, trees and diseases of all kinds—that they would do harm in no way to Balder the Beautiful.

Theirs was an easy task, for all things loved the bright Sun-god, and readily agreed to give the pledge. Nothing was overlooked save only the mistletoe, growing upon the oak-tree that shaded the entrance to Valhalla. It seemed so insignificant that no one thought it worth while to ask this plant to take the oath.

The servants returned to Frigga with all the vows and compacts that had been made; and the Mother of Gods and Men went back with heart at ease to her spinning-wheel.

The Asa folk, too, were reassured, and, casting aside the burden of care that had fallen upon them, they resumed their favourite game upon the plains of Idavold, where they were wont to contend with one another in the throwing of golden disks.

And when it became known among them that nothing would hurt Balder the Beautiful they invented a new game.

Placing the young Sun-god in their midst, they would throw stones at him, or thrust at him with their knives, or strike with their wooden staves; and the wood or the knife or the stone would glance off from Balder and leave him quite unhurt.

This new game delighted both Balder and the Asa folk, and so loud was their laughter that Loki, who was some distance away pursuing one of his schemes in the disguise of an old woman, shook with rage at the sound. For Loki was jealous of Balder and, as is usual with people who make themselves disliked, nothing gave him such displeasure as to see a group of the Asas on such happy terms with each other.

Presently, in his wanderings, Loki passed by the house of Fensalir, in the doorway of which sat Frigga, at her spinning-wheel. She did not recognise Red Loki, but greeted him kindly and asked:

"Old woman, dost thou know why the gods are so merry this evening?"

And Loki answered: "They are casting stones and throwing sharp knives and great clubs at Balder the Beautiful, who stands smiling in their midst, daring them to hurt him."

Then Frigga smiled tranquilly and turned again to her wheel, saying: "Let them play on, for no harm will come to him whom all things in heaven and earth have sworn not to hurt."

"Art thou sure, good mother, that *all* things in heaven and earth have taken this vow?"

"Ay, indeed," replied Frigga, "all save a harmless little plant, the mistletoe, which grows on the oak by Valhalla, and this is far too small and weak to be feared."

And to this Loki replied in musing voice, nodding his head as he spoke: "Yea, thou art right, great Mother of Gods and Men."

But the wicked Asa had learnt what he desired to know. The instrument by which he might bring harm to Balder the Beautiful was now awaiting him, and he determined to use it, to the dire sorrow of Asgard.

Hastening to the western gate of Valhalla, he pulled a clump of the mistletoe from the oak, and fashioned therefrom a little wand, or stick, and with this in his hand he returned to the plain of Idavold. He was far too cunning, however, to attempt to carry out his wicked design himself. His malicious heart was too well known to the Asa folk. But he soon found an innocent tool. Leaning against a tree, and taking no part in the game, was Hoder, the blind god, the twin-brother of Balder, and to him he began:

"Hark to the Asas—how they laugh! Do you take no share in the game, good Hoder?"

"Not I," said Hoder gloomily, "for I am blind, and know not where to throw."

"I could show you that," said Loki, assuming a pleasant tone; "'tis no hard matter, Hoder, and methinks the Asas will call you proud and haughty if you take no share in the fun."

"But I have nothing to throw," said poor blind Hoder.

Then Loki said: "Here, at least, is a small shaft, 'twill serve your purpose," and leading innocent Hoder into the ring he cunningly guided his aim. Hoder, well pleased to be able to share in a game with his beloved brother, boldly sped the shaft, expecting to hear the usual shouts of joyous laughter which greeted all such attempts. There fell instead dead silence on his ear, and immediately on this followed a wail of bitter agony. For Balder the Beautiful had fallen dead without a groan, his heart transfixed by the little dart of mistletoe.

> "So on the floor lay Balder dead; and round
> Lay thickly strewn swords, axes, darts, and spears,
> Which all the gods in sport had idly thrown
> At Balder, whom no weapon pierced or clove;
> But in his breast stood fixed the fatal bough
> Of mistletoe, which Loki the Accuser gave
> To Hoder, and unwitting Hoder threw—
> 'Gainst that alone had Balder's life no charm."

Dreading he knew not what, Hoder stood in doubt for some moments. But soon the meaning of that bitter wail was borne in upon him, piercing the cloud of darkness in which he always moved. He opened wide his arms as though to clasp the beloved form, and then with: "I have slain thee, my brother," despair seized him and he fell prostrate in utter grief.

Meantime, the Asa folk crowded round the silent form of Balder, weeping and wailing; but, alas! their moans and tears could not bring Balder back. At length, All-Father Odin, whose grief was too deep for lamentations, bade them be silent and prepare to bear the body of the dead Asa to the seashore.

The unhappy Hoder, unable to take part in these last offices, made his way sadly through Asgard, beyond the walls and along the seashore, until he came to the house Fensalir.

Frigga was seated upon her seat of honour before the fire against the inner wall, and standing before her, with bent head and woeful sightless gaze, Hoder told her of the dread mishap that had befallen.

"Tell me, O mother," he cried in ending, and his voice sounded like the wail of the wind on stormy nights, "tell me, is there aught I can do to bring my brother back? Or can I make agreement with the dread mother of the Underworld, giving my life in exchange for his?"

Woe crowded upon woe in the heart of Frigga as she listened to the story. The doom was wrought that she had tried so vainly to avert, and not even her mother's love had availed to safeguard the son so dearly cherished.

"On Balder Death hath laid her hand, not thee, my son," she said, "yet though we fail in the end, there is much that may be tried before all hope is lost."

Then she told Hoder of a road by which the abode of Hela could be reached, one which had been travelled by none living save Odin himself.

> "Who goes that way must take no other horse
> To ride, but Sleipnir, Odin's horse, alone.
> Nor must he choose that common path of gods
> Which every day they come and go in heaven,
> O'er the bridge Bifrost, where is Heimdall's watch.
>
> But he must tread a dark untravelled road
> Which branches from the north of heaven, and ride
> Nine days, nine nights, toward the northern ice,
> Through valleys deep engulfed, with roaring streams.
> And he will reach on the tenth morn a bridge
> Which spans with golden arches Giöll's stream.
> Then he will journey through no lighted land,
> Nor see the sun arise, nor see it set;
>
> And he must fare across the dismal ice
> Northward, until he meets a stretching wall
> Barring his way, and in the wall a grate,
> But then he must dismount and on the ice
> Tighten the girths of Sleipnir, Odin's horse,
> And make him leap the grate, and come within."

There in that cheerless abode dead Balder was enthroned, but, said Frigga, he who braves that dread journey must take no heed of him, nor of the sad ghosts flitting to and fro, like eddying leaves. First he must accost their gloomy queen and entreat her with prayers:

> "Telling her all that grief they have in heaven
> For Balder, whom she holds by right below."

A bitter groan of anguish escaped from Hoder when Frigga had finished her recital of the trials which must be undergone:

> "Mother, a dreadful way is this thou showest;
> No journey for a sightless god to go."

And she replied:

> ". . . Thyself thou shalt not go, my son;
> But he whom first thou meetest when thou com'st
> To Asgard and declar'st this hidden way,
> Shall go; and I will be his guide unseen."

Meantime the Asa folk had felled trees and had carried to the seashore outside the walls of Asgard a great pile of fuel, which they laid upon the deck of Balder's great ship, *Ringhorn,* as it lay stranded high up on the beach.

> "Seventy ells and four extended
>   On the grass the vessel's keel;
> High above it, gilt and splendid,
> Rose the figurehead ferocious
>   With its crest of steel."

Then they adorned the funeral pyre with garlands of flowers, with golden vessels and rings, with finely wrought weapons and rich necklets and armlets; and when this was done they carried out the fair body of Balder the Beautiful, and bearing it reverently upon their shields they laid it upon the pyre.

Then they tried to launch the good ship, but so heavily laden was she that they could not stir her an inch.

The Mountain-Giants, from their heights afar, had watched the tragedy with eyes that were not unpitying, for even they had no ill-will for Balder, and they sent and told of a giantess called Hyrroken, who was so strong that she could launch any vessel whatever its weight might be.

So the Asas sent to fetch her from Giantland, and she soon came, riding a wolf for steed and twisted serpents for reins.

When she alighted, Odin ordered four of his mightiest warriors to hold the wolf, but he was so strong that they could do nothing until the giantess had thrown him down and bound him fast.

Then with a few enormous strides, Hyrroken reached the great vessel, and set her shoulder against the prow, sending the ship rolling into the deep. The earth shook with the force of the movement as though with an earthquake, and the Asa folk collided with one another like pine-trees during a storm. The ship, too, with its precious weight, was well-nigh lost. At this Thor was wroth and, seizing his hammer, would have slain the giantess had not the other Asas held him back, bidding him not forget the last duty to the dead god. So Thor hallowed the pyre with a touch of his sacred hammer and kindled it with a thorn twig, which is the emblem of sleep.

Last of all, before the pyre blazed up, All-Father Odin added to the pile of offerings his magic ring, from which fell eight new rings every ninth night, and bending he whispered in Balder's ear.

But none to this day know the words that Odin spake thus in the ear of his dead son.

Then the flames from the pyre rose high and the great ship drifted out to sea, and the wind caught the sails and fanned the flames till it seemed as though sky and sea were wrapped in golden flame.

> "And while they gazed, the sun went lurid down
> Into the smoke-wrapt sea, and night came on.
> But through the dark they watched the burning ship
> Still carried o'er the distant waters. . . .
> But fainter, as the stars rose high, it flared;
> And as, in a decaying winter fire,
> A charr'd log, falling, makes a shower of sparks—
> So, with a shower of sparks, the pile fell in,
> Reddening the sea around; and all was dark."

And thus did Balder the Beautiful pass from the peaceful steads of Asgard, as passes the sun when he paints the evening clouds with the glory of his setting.

Note.—Most of the poetical extracts throughout this chapter are taken from Matthew Arnold's "Balder Dead."

THE PASSING OF BALDER

I heard a voice, that cried,
"Balder the Beautiful
Is dead, is dead!"
And through the misty air
Passed like the mournful cry
Of sunward sailing cranes.

I saw the pallid corpse
Of the dead sun
Borne through the Northern sky.
Blasts from Niffelheim
Lifted the sheeted mists
Around him as he passed.

And the voice for ever cried,
"Balder the Beautiful
Is dead, is dead!"
And died away
Through the dreary night,
In accents of despair.

Balder the Beautiful,
God of the summer sun,
Fairest of all the Gods!
Light from his forehead beamed,
Runes were upon his tongue,
As on the warrior's sword.

All things in earth and air
Bound were by magic spell
Never to do him harm;
Even the plants and stones;
All save the mistletoe,
The sacred mistletoe!

Hoder, the blind old God,
Whose feet are shod with silence,
Pierced through that gentle breast
With his sharp spear, by fraud

Made of the mistletoe,
The accursed mistletoe!

They laid him in his ship,
With horse and harness,
As on a funeral pyre.
Odin placed
A ring upon his finger,
And whispered in his ear.

They launched the burning ship!
It floated far away
Over the misty sea,
Till like the sun it seemed,
Sinking beneath the waves.
Balder returned no more!

LONGFELLOW.

CHAPTER XIII

How Hermod Made a Journey to the Underworld

This is the tale which the Northmen tell of how
Hermod journeyed to the Underworld to bring
back Balder the Beautiful to Asgard

OF all the Asa folk most fleet of foot was Hermod, but on that sad eve when Balder was laid upon the funeral pyre his step was lagging and slow as he went to his home by the city wall.

As he approached, there met him in the gloom a vague figure, that walked with outstretched hands and faltering steps like one that is blind. And Hermod knew it to be the form of Hoder of the sightless eyes, brother to Balder and to him.

But when he would have spoken Hoder brushed past, murmuring in his ear:

"Take Sleipnir, Hermod, and set forth with dawn
To Hela's kingdom, to ask Balder back;
and they shall be thy guides who have the power."

Hermod bowed his head and passed on; but poor blind Hoder, heartbroken, went his way to his own house and shut the door upon his grief.

When the first rosy fingers of dawn touched the clouds of morning Hermod led out Sleipnir, the steed of Odin, from Valhalla, and rode away. Sleipnir was not wont to permit any to mount him, or even to touch his mane, save the All-Father himself; but he stood meekly as Hermod mounted; for he knew upon what errand they were bound.

Nine long days and nine long nights rode Hermod towards the realms of ice and snow; and on the tenth morn he drew near to the golden bridge which spanned Giöll, the greatest river in the world.

A maiden of pale and downcast mien kept this bridge, with unsleeping vigilance, and she now challenged Hermod as he approached:

> "Who art thou on thy black and fiery horse,
> Under whose hoofs the bridge o'er Giöll's stream
> Rumbles and shakes? Tell me thy race and home.
> But yestermorn, five troops of dead passed by,
> Bound on their way below to Hela's realm,
> Nor shook the bridge so much as thou alone.
> And thou hast flesh and colour on thy cheeks,
> Like men who live, and draw the vital air;
> Nor look'st thou pale and wan, like men deceased,
> Souls bound below, my daily passers here."

Then Hermod told his name and whence he came, and asked eagerly if Balder had already crossed that bridge. And the maiden told him that Balder had indeed passed that way along the road to Hela's kingdom.

So Hermod galloped over the golden bridge, and resumed his way through a darksome tract of frozen country, and over fields of ice unlighted save by dim stars that shone uncertainly through the mist. At length further passage was barred by a high wall in which was a grate. Without hesitation Hermod put Sleipnir to this obstacle, he surmounted it with the ease and grace of a fawn, and they found themselves in Hela's realm.

On passed Hermod, unheeding the murmuring shades that

flocked around, and he did not draw rein until, coming to Hela's hall, he saw there Balder, his brother, and, near by, the awful goddess.

Leaping from Sleipnir, the young Asa knelt before Hela and besought her that Balder might ride home with him, that the heavy hearts of all in Asgard might be comforted.

But dark Hela shook her head, reminding him how Odin had cast her out with her two brothers, the Serpent and the Fenris Wolf; why should she grant the Asa folk this boon?

Then Hermod laid his hands upon her knees. "All things in heaven and earth grieve for Balder, therefore restore him, good mother, and darken not our lives for evermore," he answered.

The appeal in his mournful eyes, as well as in his words, somewhat moved Hela, though her heart was still hardened against Odin, and she said: "Come now, let us see if all things love Balder as you say,

> "Show me through all the world the signs of grief!
> Fails but one thing to grieve, here Balder stops!
> Let all that lives and moves upon the earth
> Weep him, and all that is without life weep:
> Let gods, men, brutes, beweep him; plants and stones.
> So shall I know the lost was dear indeed,
> And bend my heart, and give him back to heaven."

Then Hermod was given permission to greet his brother, and Balder answered him with faint voice. They spoke of Asgard, the beloved land of living gods and heroes, and at parting Balder charged his brother to carry the magic ring, Draupnir, back to Odin, and a kerchief and other gifts to Frigga, as tokens of his love. And Hermod rode sadly back along the weary road to Asgard.

All-Father Odin from his high seat saw his son returning, and he hastened forth to receive him.

> "And Hermod came, and leapt from Sleipnir down,
> And in his father's hand put Sleipnir's rein
> And greeted Odin and the gods."

Then all the Asa folk assembled in the Council Hall, at the root of the Tree of Life, to hear the message that Hermod had brought from the joyless realms; and he told them of Hela's reply to his request, saying:

> ". . . To your prayer she sends you this reply:
> *Show her through all the world the signs of grief!*
> *Fails but one thing to grieve, there Balder stops!*
> *Let gods, men, brutes, beweep him; plants and stones;*
> *So shall she know your loss was dear indeed,*
> *and bend her heart, and give you Balder back."*

When Hermod had ceased speaking, All-Father Odin arose, and leaning on his great staff he looked slowly around and commanded: "Go ye quickly forth through all the world and pray all living and unliving things to weep for Balder dead."

Then the gods arose willingly and went their way through all the world, Thor in his goat chariot, and Freya in her carriage drawn by white cats, but most of the others on swift horses. North, South, East, and West, they rode, entreating all things to weep for Balder's death.

> "And all that lived, and all without life, wept."

Just as at the end of winter, before the springtime, when a warm south-west wind blows over the land and melts the ice and snow,

> "A dripping sound is heard
> In all the forests. . . .
> And, in fields sloping to the south, dark plots
> Of grass peep out amid surrounding snow,
> And widen, and the peasant's heart is glad"—

so through the whole world was now heard the sound of falling tears, as all things living and dead wept for Balder's sake.

Hermod rode with the Storm-god, Niörd, who knew all the creeks and hidden bays of the coastline of the earth; and when the sea-creatures and those that live on the borders of the ocean heard the message they all added their tribute of tears to the common cause.

Now, as the Asas rode home together they came to a great wood upon the borders of Giantland, where all the trees are of iron. And in the midst of this wood was a cave, at the mouth of which sat an ancient giantess, gnashing her teeth at all who passed by.

This seeming giantess was none other but wicked Loki in disguise, but this Hermod did not know.

As the Asas came near, she greeted them with shrill laughter, and asked them if it was dull in Asgard that they came thither to her iron wood. But they answered that they came not for gibes but for tears, that Balder might be saved. Then she laughed louder and cried:

> "Is Balder dead? And do ye come for tears?
> Weep him all other things, if weep they will:
> I weep him not! let Hela keep her prey."

And with these mocking words she fled to the dark recesses of her cave, repeating again and again:

> "Neither in life, nor yet in death,
> Gave he me gladness.
> Let Hela keep her prey."

Heavy were the steps with which Hermod returned to Asgard, and when they had heard the news of how one creature had refused her tears, the eager faces of the Asa folk grew dark with woe, for they knew that never more would they see Balder—Balder the Beautiful.

But the future days brought peace to the tormented soul of Hoder, the innocent cause of all their grief.

For there was born to Odin a child who grew to his full size within a few short hours. And on the first day that he arrived in Asgard he fared forth with bow and arrow, and one of his shafts found mark in the heart of Hoder.

And so, from henceforth, the blind god and his twin-brother are together in the realms of Hela.

CHAPTER XIV

How Loki was Punished at Last

This is the tale the Northmen tell of how Red Loki
was punished at last for his sins

WHEN the Asas knew that it was Loki, disguised as Thok, the giant-woman, who had refused to shed the tears that would have won Balder's release, they determined to bear with his presence in Asgard no longer.

So with many a hard word and ugly look they drove him forth, bidding him never enter those gates again.

But the Asa folk were still sad and heavy of heart: for at every moment the gloom that lay over the city reminded them of the loss of their bright young Balder.

Ægir, god of the sea, saw their forlorn condition, and he prepared a great banquet in the caves of coral that lie underneath the sea, and bade all the Asas attend it as his guests.

> "That though for Balder every guest
> Was grieving yet,
> He might forget
> Awhile his woe in friendly feast."

The invitation was pleasing to the gods, and on the day appointed they came, attired in their richest cloaks of silk and satin, green and blue and yellow and purple, by a path through the waters whereby they reached the coral caves of the Sea-god.

Very beautiful were these caves. The walls and ceilings were carved with the most delicate fret-work of pink and cream and white, and a faint green light shone into them from the ocean without.

The floor was covered with the finest silver sand, encrusted with beautiful sea-shells, and the flowers with which the tables were adorned were feathery sea-weeds and glowing sea-anemones. In the midst of the floor was a mass of gold, so bright that it lighted up the whole place as though with fire.

The dishes upon the table were filled with the most delicious fish, of every kind and variety, and the gods sat down to the feast

well pleased, regretting only the absence of the well-loved
Balder, and the fact that Thor had been detained by a tempest,
which kept him busy in the regions of the dwarfs, from whence
he hoped to travel to the sea-caves directly his work was done.

Merrily went the banquet, for all the Asas were filled with
goodwill towards one another and towards their burly host, who
sat at the head of the board with his long grey beard sweeping
his broad chest.

Suddenly into the midst of this cheerful scene fell a black
shadow from the entrance to the cave; and there, red and gaunt,
and evil of countenance, stood Loki, glowering upon them all.

At first the Asas sat in silence, their anger too deep for words.
Then Odin arose and sternly bade the intruder begone.

This was the signal for a storm of hatred in words so evil that
they poisoned the air. For a time the Asas pretended not to
heed, but went on quietly with the meal. One of them even tried
to drown his speech by talking loudly to old Ægir in praise of the
servant who waited so deftly upon them all. But at the word
Loki sprang forward, knife in hand, and killed the unfortunate
serving-man before their eyes.

Then the Asa folk arose and cast out Loki with violence,
threatening him with dire punishment should he appear in their
presence again.

Resuming their seats at the interrupted feast, they made
brave efforts to appear gay and cheerful; but scarcely had they
begun to eat when Loki came creeping in again disguised as a
sea-serpent. Once in, he resumed his proper form and began as
before to revile the gods, taunting them one after another with
the mistakes which each had made, and telling his malicious stories, so that the gods were filled with dismay, and with suspicion,
each of his neighbour.

Louder and louder grew the voice of Loki, the Asas all the
time sitting as if turned to stone, and now he began to heap
abuse on the head of Sif, the fair-haired wife of Thor.

Suddenly there was heard outside the noise of goats' feet clat-
tering over the rocks, and in another moment the Thunderer
entered, brandishing his hammer about his head and crying:

"Silence, thou wicked wretch, or my mighty hammer shall put

a stop to thy prating. At one blow will I strike thy head from thy neck, and then will thy evil tongue be silenced once for all!"

But Loki did not wait for Thor to strike. Quick as light he dashed out of the cave and disappeared. He well knew that now at length he had indeed lost all hope of forgiveness.

Wandering in dismal wise about the earth, fear seized him after a time lest Odin or the Thunderer should find and slay him, in order to prevent further annoyance.

So he made his way to the mountains of the North, and there he built for himself a hut with four doors, open to every quarter of the earth, that, if need arose, he might be able to escape quickly.

He built this hut, moreover, close to a mountain side, down which rushed a mighty cataract of water. For he intended, if the Asas found him, to spring into the stream, change himself into a salmon, and so make good his escape.

But when, sitting within his cold and draughty hut, he began to consider the matter afresh, he remembered that, even if he carried out this plan, he would not yet be quite safe.

For though he could easily avoid any hook that ever was made, he would find it very difficult to evade capture if the gods should think of making a net like that which the Sea-goddess, Ran, spreads for unwary men when they are fishing or bathing in the sea, and all the time she is lurking near in some cavern on the shore, or enmeshed in the dark folds of a giant sea-weed in the ocean depths.

So much and so long did Loki brood over the thought of Ran's fishing-net, that at length he began to wonder if such a thing could really be made, and then to try to weave one out of twine as much like it as possible.

He had not quite finished his curious task when upon the mountain, just above the hut, he suddenly perceived the two mighty figures of his dreaded foes.

Knowing that their intention must be to enter his hut and make him prisoner, Loki hastily threw the half-made net upon the fire, and rushing forth he flung himself into the waterfall, where he quickly changed himself into a salmon and lurked unseen among the stones in the torrent's bed.

Meantime, the two Asas had entered the hut.

"Ho! ho!" said Odin, as he noted the silence of the place, "our bird has flown."

"What fresh mischief doth he plan?" muttered Thor, looking closely about him.

"Let us look further afield," urged Odin; but Thor kicked over the logs on the hearth and picked out the half-burned net.

Now Odin well knew the net of Ran, and the half-burnt strands suggested to him the truth. So he set to work and, with Thor's assistance, quickly mended the net, and they proceeded to drag the mountain stream with it.

At their first attempt sly Loki hid between two stones at the bottom of the river, laughing in scorn as the net passed over his head.

Then the Asas weighted the net with stones and tried again; but Loki gave a great leap over the net, and dashed up stream.

A third they made the attempt, and now Loki, grown reckless, leaped out of the water. But this time Thor caught him by his tail, and held it fast in spite of its slipperiness.

Then the gods forced him to resume his usual shape, and they carried him off to an underground cavern, far below the earth, and there they bound him fast to a rock with iron fetters.

Most things in heaven and earth rejoiced at the downfall of wicked Red Loki, but above all rejoiced Skadi the giantess. Her home was in the cold mountain stream which Loki had invaded, and he had done her many an ill turn in bygone days.

This Skadi now took a poisonous serpent and fastened it above his head, so that the venom of the reptile falling, drop by drop, upon his face, would cause the most terrible pain. But Sigyn, Loki's loyal wife, the only person in heaven or earth who cared what became of him, took a cup and held it up to catch the burning drops as they fell, and she only left his side when the cup was full and she had to empty it.

In these brief periods, the fettered god howled with rage and pain, in tones which echoed through the dismal caverns of earth like mighty peals of thunder, and his writhing shook the earth to its foundations, bringing the Northmen from their dwellings in terror of what they thought to be violent earthquakes.

But his efforts can avail nothing until the day of Ragnarok.

Then shall his bonds be loosed, and he shall fight his last battle and fall, never to rise again.

CHAPTER XV

The Story of the Magic Sword

This is the tale the Northmen tell of how a great feud arose between the Volsungs and the Goths

SIGI, the son of Odin, was a man mighty in the hunt, and he lived in the house of Skadi. And one day he went out to the woods with Bredi, Skadi's servant, and they hunted deer all day long. But when they gathered their spoil in the evening, it was found that Bredi had slain far more than Sigi, and it vexed the soul of Sigi that a servant should hunt better than his master. So, in his jealous rage, he fell upon Bredi and killed him, and hid his body in a snowdrift, after which he rode home in the gloaming, with the tale that Bredi had ridden away from him into the wild woods.

"Out of the sight of mine eyes he rode," said he, "and I know not what has become of him."

But Skadi did not believe his words—for Sigi's eyes looked sideways as he spoke—and he sent and searched the woods, and the body of Bredi was found in a snowdrift. Then, his dark suspicion being confirmed, he took Sigi and put him forth from the land and commanded that he be an outlaw for ever.

Sigi embarked upon the ocean in a small boat, and he had not been sailing long when a little skiff drew near, wherein was an old man with one eye, wearing a broad-brimmed grey hat. This was none other than Odin, who had come to succour his son, and he took the boat in tow and brought Sigi to a war vessel manned with a brave crew, well armed and provided, which he gave into his charge, promising that victory in battle should always be his.

Then Sigi took fresh heart and, ever aided by the powerful favour of Odin, he won at length dominion and lordship over the great empire of the Huns.

Yet did he not escape punishment for the evil deed of his youth, for when he was very old the favour of Odin forsook him; and the brother of his wife, whom he trusted above all men, fell upon him with treachery and slew him.

But the son of Sigi was now a brave youth, and gathering the warriors of his land he drove out his mother's kindred and took the kingdom for himself. When peace had settled upon it he took unto him a wife, and Frigga blessed them with a fine little son, whom they named Volsung. But while the boy was yet quite young Rerir, his father, went out to the wars and was killed, and the Battle Maidens carried him away to Odin and the festal halls of Valhalla.

The young Volsung grew mightily in valour and in strength, so that when he had come to man's estate his renown was greater than that of his father or grandfather, and all men knew him to be a true son of the race of Odin.

So in due time he became the founder of a great family, and the builder of a mighty house. The walls of his dwelling were hung with battle shields taken from the foe, and in the midst of the floor

"Sprang up a mighty tree
That reared its blessings roofward, and wreathed the roof-tree dear
With the glory of the summer and the garland of the year."

Underneath the branches of this gigantic "Branstock," as the tree was named, dwelt Volsung and his wife and their eleven children. Ten stalwart sons had he and one fair daughter, Signy by name.

Now when Signy was become a tall and stately maiden, it came to pass that Siggeir, King of the Goths, sent messages to beg that she might be given to him in marriage. And because Volsung had heard a good report of his success in war, he promised his daughter to him without setting eyes upon his face.

But when he came to claim the promise, Signy saw that her bridegroom was small and dark and evil of countenance, different indeed from the tall, fair, open-faced Northmen, and her heart sank within her.

The sacred pledge had been given, however, and no Northland maiden could draw back from the plighted word.

True to her hero-blood, Signy went through the marriage ceremony with seeming cheerfulness, and none but her twin-brother Sigmund knew her grief.

The wedding feast was celebrated with magnificence. Great fires burned brightly along the hall, and the flickering flames cast a lurid glow upon the huge oak which upreared its massive and fantastic shape in the centre.

Now, while the merry-making was at its height, there suddenly entered a tall, old man with hat slouched over his eyes and huge grey cloak around his majestic shoulders.

Advancing to the Branstock, he drew his sword, and plunged it to the very hilt in the great trunk.

Then, as the assembled guests gazed at him in awe-struck silence, he said: "Whoso draweth the sword from this stock shall have the same as a gift from me, and it shall give him victory in every battle."

There was something so attractive in the voice and mien of the speaker that all men sat chained to their seats, as in a dream. And none roused himself as the old man turned and passed through the hall and out of the door.

But as soon as Odin, for he it was, had vanished, all tongues were loosed and there arose a great hubbub. And the men of noblest rank went up one after another to the Branstock and pulled and tugged and strained at the goodly sword. First of all went up King Siggeir, but though he pulled till his eyes nearly started from his head, yet the sword moved not an inch.

Then Volsung put his hand to the sword, but it was not meant for him. Neither could the Volsung princes, who followed one by one, do aught to move it, until last of them came Sigmund, the youngest, and as soon as he grasped the hilt he pulled the weapon out of the trunk as if it had lain loose therein.

It was indeed a weapon worthy of the gods, and when Siggeir looked upon its shapely proportions his heart was fired with desire, and he offered to buy it from the youth at thrice its weight in gold.

But Sigmund answered: "Thou mightst have taken the sword

as easily as I if it had been thy lot to wear it. But now it has fallen to me, thou shalt never have it, though thou dost offer all the gold thou hast."

And thus began the fatal quarrel between the race of Siggeir and the Volsungs, for at the words Siggeir's heart grew bitter against Sigmund; and he determined that, when the time was ripe, he would put an end to the Volsung race and take that sword to himself.

But outwardly Siggeir was all that was fair and gentle. And when he set sail with his bride to his own land, he begged King Volsung and his sons to visit him as soon as possible.

So, at an appointed time, King Volsung and his ten stalwart sons set off to the kingdom of Siggeir with three brave ships; and after a fair voyage they cast anchor late one eventide.

During the night, as they lay on their ships, thinking to land next morning, Signy, who had received tidings of their arrival, came in secret to her father and brothers and begged them not to go ashore, saying that her treacherous husband had laid an ambush for them, whence they could not escape alive. She bade them therefore return to their own land, and together, with a mighty army, come again to take revenge upon King Siggeir.

But the brave old Volsung shook his great white head, saying that never yet had he or his turned back before fire or sword or hurt—and he would not play the coward in his old age.

"A hundred fights have I fought," said he, "and ever I had the victory, nor shall it be said of me that I fled from a foe or prayed for peace."

Then Signy wept right sore, and prayed that she might stay with her kinsmen, and not return to her husband.

But this seemed not good in the eyes of Volsung, and he sent her back sadly to her home.

As soon as it was day, King Volsung went ashore with his folk, and all were fully armed. But that availed them little; for Siggeir fell upon them with a great army. The Volsungs were few in number, but they fought with desperate courage, and no fewer than eight times did they cut their way through their foes. They would have done so yet again, had not Volsung fallen in the midst of his folk, and his followers with him, save only his ten sons.

Then the princes were taken and led, fast bound, into the

presence of Siggeir, who had watched the fight from afar; and when he had secured the sword of Odin he condemned the young men to die.

But Signy, wild with grief, besought her husband: "I will not pray thee to spare their lives, but let them be first set awhile in the forest, chained fast to a fallen oak; for there comes to me an old saying—'*Sweet to eye while eye can see.*' I pray not for longer life for them, because well I know that my prayer will avail nothing."

At this Siggeir laughed an evil laugh: "Surely thou art mad," he said, "to wish that the suffering of thy brothers should be prolonged. I care not, however, for the more pain they have to bear the better shall I be pleased."

So the ten young men were chained to an oak in the woods with a heavy beam upon their feet, and Signy meantime was shut up in the palace under close watch, lest she should try to succour them.

Now it came to pass that at midnight there came up a great she-wolf out of the wild woods, and she fell upon one of the brothers and devoured him and went upon her way.

Next morning Signy sent a trusty servant to bring tidings of her brothers, and grievously she mourned when she heard that one was dead; for she feared that the same fate would overtake all.

Every morning she sent the man to the forest, and every morning he returned with the news that the she-wolf had eaten up another of the Volsung princes, until all save Sigmund were dead. Then Signy, in dire despair, bethought herself of a plan, and she sent the messenger with honey in his hand to her twin-brother, and bade him smear it over Sigmund's face and feet and a little of it in his mouth. And it was done as she commanded.

And that same night, as Sigmund sat alone in the wild woods, the she-wolf came up, according to her wont, and would have slain and eaten him like his brothers. But first she smelt the honey and began to lick his face all over, and finally thrust her tongue into his mouth.

Then Sigmund caught the she-wolf's tongue in his strong teeth and held fast to it; and she, in her pain and terror, set her feet against the beam and against the oak, and strained so mightily that beam and oak gave way, and the chain that bound the prince snapped in twain. And springing up, he killed the murderer of his brothers, that gaunt she-wolf, and ran through the wild woods a free man.

Now when Signy knew what had happened she was full of joy; and as her husband thought that all the Volsungs were dead, and so kept watch over her no longer, she was able to visit her brother where he lay hiding in secret. Together they built for him a hut underground in the wild woods, and they covered up the entrance with branches, moss, and leaves, so that it was quite hidden from sight. To this retreat Signy brought food and all things that were needed, and together in secret they made plans to revenge their father and his nine brave sons.

Now to Siggeir and Signy had been born two sons who, both in nature and in face, were exactly like their father. When the eldest was ten years of age, his mother sent him to Sigmund, that he might be trained by a Volsung to avenge the death of his grandfather.

Late at eventide he came to the earth-dwelling, and when Sigmund had welcomed the boy he bade him make ready the bread for their evening meal. "For I," said he, "must go seek firewood." And with these words he gave the meal bag into his hands and left the hut.

But he could see no trace of any bread making when he came back, so he asked if the food was ready.

"No," said the boy, "I dared not set hand in the meal sack, because I saw something move in the meal."

Then Sigmund knew that the boy had the heart of a mouse, and he sent him back to his mother.

The next winter Signy sent her second son to him, and Sigmund tested him in like manner. But he too showed his coward's heart, and was sent home again.

As time went on Signy had another son, whom she called Sinfiotli. He was tall and strong and fair of face, like unto the Volsungs; and before he was ten years of age, she sent him to Sigmund. But first she tested him herself by sewing his shirt to his skin and then suddenly snatching it off again, whereat the child did but laugh at her, saying: "Full little would a Volsung care for such a smart as that."

So the boy came to Sigmund, who bade him knead the meal while he went to fetch firewood.

This time the bread stood ready baked upon the hearth when he came back, whereupon he asked Sinfiotli if he had found nothing in the meal.

"Ay," said the boy, "I saw there was something living in the meal when I first began to knead it; but I have kneaded all together, both the meal and whatever was therein."

Then Sigmund gave a great laugh, and caught the boy in his arms, saying: "Naught wilt thou eat of this bread to-night, for thou hast kneaded up therewith the most deadly of serpents."

Though no sting from outside could harm Sinfiotli, he could neither eat nor drink venom and live. But Sigmund could eat of the bread, since no poison could harm him.

From that day the training of the lad became Sigmund's constant care, and he grudged no pains in the effort to make him worthy of a Volsung's teaching.

In his desire to make him hardy and daring beyond his years he took Sinfiotli with him on all his expeditions. Together they lived the wild life of outlaws, faring far and wide through the woods, and slaying men for their wealth. And the boy forgot his father and thought as a Volsung.

Now it befell that on a day, as they roamed through the woods, they came upon a certain house, wherein lay two men, with great gold rings on wrists and ankles, fast asleep. Over their heads hung the skins of two grey wolves, and by this Sigmund knew that they were king's sons who had been turned into werewolves. Every tenth night would they come out of their wolf skins and return to them again at dawn.

Then did Sigmund and Sinfiotli, half in jest, put on the wolf skins while the men lay asleep; and having done this they could in nowise rid themselves of them till the appointed time. They rushed forth howling as wolves howl, though each knew the meaning of the sound, and they lay out in the wild woods all that night.

Next morning each prepared to go his separate way to seek food, and first they made a compact that they would risk the attack of seven men; but if more set upon them, each would howl for the other in wolfish wise.

"For thou art young and over-bold," said Sigmund, "and men will think well of themselves when they take thee."

Then each went his way, but before Sigmund had gone far he was attacked by a band of eight men. Then he gave forth the long wolf howl, and Sinfiotli came and slew them all, and returned his way again.

A few hours later eleven men met Sinfiotli in the woods and tried to kill him, but he fought them in such wise that they were all slain. Then, being weary, he crawled under an oak to take his rest. Soon came Sigmund, and seeing the dead men lying on the ground, he asked: "Why didst thou not call for help?"

But Sinfiotli only yawned and said: "I was loth to call on thee to help me slay so few as eleven men."

These words so offended Sigmund that he sprang upon Sinfiotli and bit him in the throat so sorely that he lay dead upon the ground.

Then was Sigmund heavy at heart, for he had grown to love the boy, and he cursed the wolf skin, from which he could not get free. With much difficulty, however, he succeeded in dragging the body to the hut, where he crouched beside it, howling for grief.

Now, as he sat, he saw two weasels come from behind a tree, and one bit the other in the throat, so that it lay to all appearance dead upon the ground. Then the first weasel ran into a thicket and brought a leaf in its mouth and laid it upon the wound; and immediately its companion sprang up and scampered off, perfectly cured. A moment later a raven, in his flight overhead, dropped a leaf of the same kind at Sigmund's feet.

Then he knew that Odin had sent to his aid, and he took the leaf and drew it over Sinfiotli's hurt, and the lad sprang up quite well and strong again.

So they lay down together in their earth-house till the time came to put off their wolf skins; and then they burnt them with fire and prayed the Asa folk to let no further harm come through the spell of the evil shapes.

Now when Sinfiotli was grown to manhood, Sigmund having tried him fairly and found him of true Volsung blood, plotted with him to avenge his kinsmen and exact the penalty from King Siggeir. Wherefore, on a certain day they left the earth-house and came to the palace of the king; and they gained, unperceived, a lurking-place amongst the casks of ale which were stacked in the entrance to the hall.

Now Signy and the king were sitting in the hall, and two of their younger children were trundling a golden ball along the floor. Suddenly a golden ring came off the ball and rolled behind the casks of ale, and the little ones ran after it and discovered the two big, grim men with helmets on their heads and swords in their hands.

Screaming with fright the children rushed to their father with news of what they had seen.

Then the king summoned his warriors, and a rush was made to where Sigmund and Sinfiotli lay hidden. They were quickly surrounded; and though they fought desperately, they were taken and fast bound.

That night the king pondered what would be the worst and most lingering death he could mete out to them; and when morning came he ordered a great hollow mound of stones and turf to be made, with a large flat stone, extending from wall to wall, in the midst; and he ordered the prisoners to be buried alive, one on each side of this stone, so that they could hear each other speak but might in nowise pass through to one another.

Now, while the servants were closing in the mound, came Signy along with a bundle of straw in her arms, and this she cast down to Sinfiotli, bidding the men say nothing of this to the king; and they promised, and set the topmost stones, and left the two to die.

Presently Sinfiotli called to Sigmund and said: "I at anyrate shall not starve for awhile, for the queen has thrown in a lump of swine's flesh wrapped in straw."

A moment later he gave a shout of joy, for hidden in the meat he found the magic sword of Sigmund, which he knew by the hilt, for Sigmund had often talked to him of this weapon.

He now drove the point with all his strength into the big stone, and it passed quite through, so that Sigmund caught the point and pulled to and fro; and in this wise they sawed right through that mighty stone, and stood together in the mound. But they stayed not there, for with that good sword they soon cut their way through stones and iron and turf.

Then, very softly, they crept to the king's hall where all men slept, and set wood around it; and having secured the door they set fire to the wood.

It was not long ere the folk within were awakened by the smoke and flames, and the king cried out: "Who kindled this fire in which I burn?"

"I," replied Sigmund, "with Sinfiotli, my sister's son, that you may know well that all the Volsungs are not yet dead."

Then he entreated his sister to come out into a place of safety; but she would not. "Merrily now will I die with King Siggeir, though I was not merry to wed him," said she, and she perished in the fire with her husband and his men.

Sigmund and Sinfiotli now gathered together folk and ships and returned to the land of the Volsungs, where they were warmly welcomed.

And thus ended the great feud between the Volsungs and the Goths.

CHAPTER XVI

How Sigmund Fought His Last Battle

This is the tale the Northmen tell of how Sigmund took Hiordis to wife, and was slain of the might of Odin

N OW Sigmund in course of time became the greatest king of all the Volsungs; and Sinfiotli was the captain of his host.

And it came to pass that Sinfiotli loved a fair woman and desired to have her for his wife; but the brother of Sigmund's queen was also in love with her. So they fought together in a distant land, and Sinfiotli slew his rival.

Many another battle did he fight, until he had become renowned above all men; and in the autumn-tide he turned home again.

And when he had told all his news to King Sigmund he went to the queen, and told how he had slain her brother in fair fight. Now when she heard this the queen was wroth, and bade him begone from the kingdom, nor would she listen to his words about the quarrel. But Sigmund forbade him to depart, and, declaring that her brother had been slain in fair fight, offered to his wife much gold in atonement for the unhappy deed.

Then the queen, seeing that her will was not likely to prevail, bowed her head, and said: "Have thy way in this matter, my lord, for it is right that so it should be."

But in her heart she harboured evil thoughts against Sinfiotli. Then she held a funeral feast for her dead brother, and bade thither many great men.

And at that feast, as was the custom in those days, the queen carried horns of mead to the chief guests. And when she came to Sinfiotli in his turn she put the mighty horn into his hands, saying, with a smile: "Come now and drink, fair nephew."

But Sinfiotli looked therein and said: "Nay; for there is a charm within the mead."

"Give it to me," quoth Sigmund, when he heard those words. And he took the horn and drank off the mead.

But the queen's face darkened, and she taunted Sinfiotli, saying: "Must other men quaff thy drink for thee?"

And she came a second time and gave the horn into his hands, saying: "Art thou a coward after all? Come now and drink."

But he looked into the horn, and lo: "Guile is in the drink," said he.

Sigmund again seized the vessel, saying: "Give it then to me," and drank the full draught.

Then the queen came to Sinfiotli a third time, and mocked him, saying: "How is this that thou fearest to take thy mead like a man? If thou hast the heart of a Volsung, drink now thy portion."

But again he looked on the horn, and said: "Venom is therein."

Now Sigmund by this time was weary of drinking, and he said: "Pour it through thy beard then, and all will be well." But Sinfiotli mistook his meaning, and thought he desired him to drink the mead; and he drank, and straightway fell down dead to the ground.

Then the heart of Sigmund was full of grief at his kinsman's end. He would let no man touch him, but took him in his arms and fared away to the wild woods and so to the seashore. And behold, there was an old man sitting in a little boat; on his head was a grey hat pulled well over his face, and over his shoulders a blue-grey cloak.

"Wilt thou be ferried across the bay?" asked the old man; and Sigmund bowed his head. But the boat was too little to carry all at once; so Sinfiotli was laid therein and Sigmund stood by on the shore.

A moment later both boat and ferryman had vanished from before his eyes.

Then Sigmund knew that All-Father Odin had himself come for his kinsman and had carried him to the halls of Asgard, and, after he had mused awhile upon what had befallen, he returned to his folk; but because of the wrong that she had done he would not look upon his queen again, and soon afterwards she died.

Now there lived in a neighbouring kingdom a mighty and famous king, who had a daughter named Hiordis; and she was the fairest and wisest of women. And it came to pass that King Sigmund heard it told of her that she was the only woman who was fitted to be his wife; and he made a journey to the court of the king her father, and looked on her and loved her. And her father listened graciously to his proposal that he should marry his daughter.

But at that same time King Lygni, son of Hunding; and he also demanded the hand of Hiordis in marriage. And the king, fearful lest trouble should come, called his daughter, and said: "Full wise art thou, my daughter, and it is fitting that thou alone shalt choose thy husband. Say now which of these two kings thou wilt have, and I will abide by thy choice."

And Hiordis said: "I will chose King Sigmund, though he is old and stricken in years, for the greater valour has been his."

So to him she was betrothed, and King Lygni was obliged to depart. And in due time a great wedding feast was made, and Sigmund and Hiordis were married with all the rites customary in the Northland, after which they returned to Sigmund's own kingdom.

But within a few months news was brought that King Lygni had gathered together a vast army, and was marching upon the Volsungs with intent to destroy them utterly. So King Sigmund hastily got together his fighting men and went out to his enemy, and they met in an open space in the middle of a wood. And

Hiordis carried away the king's treasure and hid herself in the wood with her handmaid, in a place from whence she could watch the fight.

The Vikings that came up from the sea were greater in number by far than the warriors of Sigmund. But Sigmund was a host in himself, and all the fierce strength of the Volsungs was in his arm that day. Wherever he went his foes made way before him, and full many were the Vikings who fell by his magic sword. But the king, who was the father of his wife, was killed in the foremost rank.

Now, when the battle had raged for a long time, suddenly a strange warrior, tall of form, with slouched hat upon his head, and blue-grey cloak about his shoulders, was seen making his way through the press to where Sigmund towered above the host of those who came against him. Soon he confronted Sigmund, and his flashing weapon whirled like a flail ere it descended. The Volsung king lifted his magic sword to ward off the blow, but it fell with terrific force upon the blade and broke it in two pieces. From that moment the fortune of the battle turned against the Volsungs, and they fell fast around their king. But Sigmund stood as in a trance, and the war rage faded from his face. All-Father Odin had come to claim the sword he had given all those many years ago, and had left him defenceless against the foe who now pressed hot upon him.

"And there they smote down Sigmund, the wonder of all lands,
  On the foemen, on the death-heap his deeds had piled that day."

When he saw that his rival had fallen, King Lygni made for the king's abode, meaning to take both queen and treasure for himself. But he found all empty and silent within. Then, thinking that he had slain every one of the Volsung race, and that he need dread them no more, he went through the kingdom to take possession of it.

When night had fallen upon the scene of bloodshed, Hiordis crept out of the thicket and searched among the dead for her beloved Sigmund. Presently she found him lying, and the life was still in him; and taking him in her arms she thought to staunch his wounds. But with faint voice he said: "War have I

waged as long as it was Odin's will, but never will I draw sword
again, since the blade he gave me has broken in two. My good
fortune has departed, and I will not suffer myself to be healed."

Then Hiordis wept sore and answered: "Naught would I care
if but one Volsung was left to avenge thee and my father."

And Sigmund said: "A son shall be born to thee who shall be
mightier than I. Our boy shall be the noblest and most famed of
all the Volsung race. See to it that thou keep the pieces of my
good sword, for from it he shall fashion a goodly blade, and shall
work many a great work therewith, and his name shall abide and
flourish as long as the world shall endure.

"But now am I weary, and would fain go to join my kindred
that have gone before me."

All through the night Hiordis kept watch beside him, till, at
the dawn, he died.

And as the queen mourned over the lifeless body she heard
the sound of many ships upon the seashore, and she said to her
handmaid: "Let us now exchange garments and flee into the
woods, and do thou play the part of king's daughter, and I will
be thy handmaid."

Then there came up a great band of Vikings from the shore,
and their leader was Alf, son of the King of Denmark. And they
saw how a great company of men lay slain, and also how two
women had escaped into the woods.

So Alf bade his followers go seek the maidens, and bring them
before him. This they did, and when he questioned them, the
handmaid spoke as though she were queen, and answered for
both, and told of the fall of King Sigmund, and who it was who
had brought the war trouble into the land.

Then the prince asked if they knew where the wealth of the
king was hidden, and the maiden replied: "Ay, we know full well
where it is laid."

And she guided them to the place, and this pleased the
prince, and he put the treasure aboard his ships, and took the
women also with him. But first he gave ear to the tale of Sigmund,
and it won his admiration, and he caused the king to be buried
as beseemed his rank and valour.

Then did Hiordis and the handmaid sail away with Alf to his
own land.

CHAPTER XVII

The Story of the Magic Gold

*This is the tale the Northmen tell of how
Sigurd was nurtured in Denmark*

WHEN Hiordis and her handmaid came to the kingdom of Prince Alf, they were treated with all honour and goodwill. But soon the queen-mother of Prince Alf called him to her and said:

"Tell me, my son, why the fairer of these women has the fewer rings and the commoner garments? For methinks that she whom you have held of least account is the nobler of the two."

And he answered: "I, too, have had my doubts, since she is little like a bond-servant, and when we first met she greeted me in noble wise. But let us make trial of the matter."

So it came to pass that, as they sat at table, the prince said: "How is it that you know the hour for rising in the winter mornings, seeing that there are then no lights in heaven?"

And the handmaid, who was playing the part of mistress, forgot herself, and answered: "At a certain hour I was ever wont to drink milk before wending to feed the cows; and now that I no longer do this, I still awake thereby at that self-same time."

At this the prince laughed aloud, saying: "That is ill manners for a king's daughter."

Then he turned to Hiordis and asked her the same question, and she answered unthinkingly: "My father once gave me a little gold ring of such a nature that it grows cold on my finger in the daydawning; and that is the sign by which I know it is time to rise."

Then the prince sprang up, saying: "Gold rings for a bondmaid! Come now, thou has deceived me, for I perceive that thou art a king's daughter."

So the queen told him the whole truth, and then was she held in the greatest honour.

Soon after, Prince Alf succeeded to his father's throne and became King of Denmark, and about this time a fair son was given to Hiordis, as had been foretold by Sigmund, his father. His hair was fair as the morning light and his eyes were keen and blue.

And when, as happened shortly afterwards, the king married

Hiordis, the young Sigurd, as he was named, was brought up at the palace, with all care and love, as the king's foster-son. Tall and straight did he grow, and very comely of countenance; and there was no man but loved him.

In due time the young prince was sent to Regin, the wisest man in that realm, to be taught by him.

So old was he that none could recall his first coming to the land, and his wisdom embraced all things known to men. He had great skill in all the arts of peace, but chiefly was he famed for the mighty works he had wrought at the forge and upon the anvil.

> "The Master of the Masters in the smithying craft was he;
>   And he dealt with the wind and the weather and the stilling of
>   the sea."

But though he was so wise, he had an evil heart, and he soon determined to use the young Sigurd for his own ends.

So one day he began to instil a spirit of discontent within the lad, asking him if he knew how much wealth his father Sigmund had and who now had it in charge.

And the boy answered: "The king himself has it in charge."

"Dost thou then trust him so utterly?" sneered Regin.

"It is but right he should have it so," answered Sigurd, "for he knows better how to guard it than I."

So Regin waited awhile, and then tried again, saying: "Surely it is a marvellous thing that thou, a king's son, should run about on thy feet like a horse-boy, and do the bidding of King Alf!"

"That is not so," said Sigurd, "for I have my way in all things, and whatever I desire is granted to me."

"Well, then," said Regin, "ask for a horse for thyself."

"Yes," said the boy; "and that shall I have when I have need of such a thing."

After this Sigurd went to the king, who smiled on him and said: "What wilt thou of me?"

And Sigurd said: "I would have a horse of my very own."

To which the king replied: "Choose for thyself a horse from any part of the kingdom it seems good to thee."

So Sigurd went away to the wild woods to consider where he should search for the finest steed in all the world; and as he pondered he met in the way a tall, old man, with a grey hat drawn over his forehead and a grey-blue cloak about his shoulders, who asked him where he was going.

"I want to choose a horse," said Sigurd. "Come thou with me, old man, and give me thy counsel."

So they went together to a meadow where all the finest horses in the king's dominions were feeding, in charge of the royal grooms. And the stranger said: "See now, let us drive all these horses into the deeps of the river and choose the one that best can cross the foaming tide."

And this they did. And it came to pass that, because of the strong swirl of the waters, all but one of the horses turned back and scrambled again to land.

But one not only breasted the tide as though it were still water, but, having gained the opposite bank, he raced round the meadow as though he were a colt. Then plunging into the river again he swam back quite easily and rejoined his companions.

"That is the horse that I will choose," said young Sigurd, and running out, he caught the beautiful creature by the mane. Young of years was he, grey of colour, and very great and fair of limb; and as yet no man had thrown foot across his back.

Then said the old man: "This horse is of the kin of Sleipnir, the steed of Odin. Nourish him well, for he will prove the best of horses to thee."

And with those words he vanished.

Then Sigurd called the steed Greyfell, and he proved, as Odin had promised, the best of all horses in the world.

And after awhile Regin spoke again to Sigurd and said: "It grieves me sore to see thee in this poor and humble guise at the court. But thou art a brave lad, and I will tell thee where there is much wealth to be won, as well as fame and honour in the winning of it, if thou wilt."

These words roused Sigurd's curiosity, and he asked where that wealth might be, and who had watch and ward over it.

And Regin answered: "Fafnir is his name, and he lies not so far away, on a lonely waste of heath. And when thou comest to that place, thou mayest well say that thou hast never seen or heard of such abundance of treasure."

"But I have already heard of Fafnir," said Sigurd thoughtfully.

"Is he not the most terrible of dragons, so huge and evil that no man dare go out against him?"

"Not so," said the cunning Regin, "he is like unto other dragons of his kind. Men make too great a tale about him, that is all. But there, thy forefathers would have thought nothing of such a beast, but 'tis hardly to be expected that thou, though thou be of Volsung blood, shalt have the heart and mind of those great ones whose deeds of fame still ring throughout the lands."

Then Sigurd grew angry. "Why shouldst thou lay on me the name of coward, who am yet but a child?" he said. "I have had as yet no chance to win renown. And tell me, why dost thou egg me on to this so strongly?"

"Hundreds of years ago," replied Regin, "when I was but a boy, I lived in the house of my father Hreidmar, the king of the dwarfs. His eldest son was named Fafnir, his second Otter, and I was the youngest and least; for I could never wield a sword in battle, though I was a cunning worker in iron and silver and gold. My brother Otter was cleverer than I, for he was a great fisher, and excelled all other men as such.

"By day he took the form of an otter, and dwelt in the river, and brought fish in his mouth to the bank. He lived usually thus, coming home only to eat and slumber, for on dry land he could see nothing. But Fafnir was by far more grim, as he was greater than us all, and he would have everything we possessed called his.

"Now in the waterfall hard by our house lived a dwarf called Andvari, who had changed himself into the likeness of a pike; and this he did that he might eat the smaller fishes, of which the river was full.

"And one day it came to pass that three of the Asa folk, Odin, Loki, and Hœnir, being on a journey, came to Andvari's waterfall just as Otter, having eaten a large salmon, was slumbering on the river bank. When Loki saw him he took up a stone, and threw it with such force that my brother fell dead on the ground. At this the Asas were well content, for they did not know that he was a dwarf's son. And they flayed off his skin and Loki carried it away with him, hanging it over his shoulder.

"Now at eventide they came to the house of my father, and entered in, suspecting no evil. But when Loki, coming last, threw his burden on the floor, the dwarf king recognised the skin, and his face grew black with rage. Before the Asas could defend themselves or flee, he made signs to his servants who bound them fast in the midst of the floor.

"Then the Asas asked what ransom they should pay, and Hreidmar answered and said: 'In the depth of the waterfall lies the Flame of the Waters, the Gold of the Sea, hidden there by the dwarfs, and called by men Andvari's Hoard. Find this for me, and fill with it the otter skin, and cover it outside with the same red gold, and then, and then only, will I let you go free.'

"Now this was a heavy ransom indeed, for not only was Andvari's hoard hidden cunningly away, but the otter skin had the property of stretching itself to an enormous size.

"The Asas, however, determined to do their best, and they sent Loki, who was set free for the purpose, to find the Magic Gold.

"So Loki went down to the river bank and peered and poked and searched. This he did for days, but nowhere could he discover either the dwarf Andvari or his hoard. At length he noticed a wonderfully fine pike, with gills of gold, which each day sported in the foam of the waterfall, and he suspected that this was the dwarf in the form of a fish.

"So he went to Ran, the goddess of the sea, and borrowed her magic net, and taking this to the waterfall he cast it therein; and the pike swam into the net and was caught. Then said Loki:

> 'What fish of all fishes
> Swims strong in the flood,
> But hath learnt little wit to unfold?
> Thine head must thou buy
> If fate thou would'st fly,
> And find me the water's red gold.'

"The dwarf now resumed his proper form, and answered sulkily:

> 'Andvari folk call me,
> A dwarf is my father,
> And deep in the fall is my home.
> For of ill-luck a fay
> This fate on me lay,
> Through wet ways ever to roam.'

"Slowly, and very reluctantly, the dwarf accepted the situation; but at last he consented to yield up the golden hoard as ransom for his life, and diving into the depths of the waterfall he brought up thence, little by little, his marvellous pile of treasure.

"Last of all he laid upon the bank, which now shone like a sea of gold, the glittering Helmet of Dread and a massive breast-plate, all of the precious metal.

"'This is the full measure,' said he, as he laid his burden at Loki's feet.

"But Loki caught sight of a ring gleaming upon his thumb. 'Give me also that ring,' said he.

"Now this ring was a talisman and had the power of attracting to it all precious metal like itself; therefore Andvari would not part with it.

"Then Loki snatched the ring from him with a wicked laugh, and went his way chuckling. But Andvari crept into a cleft of the rocks, and from thence called out angry curses upon him.

> 'That gold hoard of mine
> Shall be to all thine
> A cause of dissension and woe;
> And no good at all
> Shall ever befall
> The man to whose hands it shall go.'

"Meanwhile, Loki had carried the treasure to Hreidmar, and they placed it on the otter skin, which ever stretched and widened, so that, with all that large store, one hair of the bristle remained uncovered. And on this Loki placed the magic ring, that was called 'Andvari's Loom,' because it made much gold, and at last the skin was entirely covered. Then Loki chanted:

> 'Gold enow, gold enow,
> A great treasure hast thou,
> That our heads on our necks we may hold,
> But thou and thy son,
> Are now both undone,
> For a curse has been placed on the gold.'

"Now scarcely had the Asas departed than the curse began to work. For though Hreidmar watched night and day over the treasure, it was plain that Fafnir coveted it. At last he slew his father, and having thus obtained possession of the hoard he donned the Helmet of Dread and the glittering breastplate, and," said Regin, "he drove me out when I came to claim my share, and bade me get my bread as best I could.

"And so evil did Fafnir grow with gloating over the treasure, begrudging any man a share in his wealth, that he took the shape of a vile dragon, and to this day he lies brooding over his hoard.

"As for me, I went to the king, who made me master smith."

"Hast thou hearkened, Sigurd? Wilt thou help a man that is old
To avenge him for his father? Wilt thou win the treasure of gold
And be more than the kings of the earth? Wilt thou rid the earth
    of a wrong
And heal the woe and the sorrow my heart hath endured o'er
    long?"

Then Sigurd answered: "Much wrong has been thine and exceeding evil has thy kinsman been to thee. Make me, therefore, a sword by thy craft, such as none has ever been made before; and with it I will go forth to slay this mighty dragon."

"Trust me well in that task," said Regin, "and with that same sword shalt thou slay Fafnir."

CHAPTER XVIII

How Sigurd Slew the Dragon

*This is the tale the Northmen tell of how Sigurd slew
Fafnir and Regin with the Magic Sword*

REGIN set to work, and exercising all his skill as a cunning worker in metals he fashioned a sword, very fine and keen and strong, and this he brought to Sigurd.

Sigurd received it with joy, but the weapon which was to slay Fafnir must be severely tested; and, raising it aloft, the youth smote with all his might upon the iron anvil, and the sword broke in pieces.

"Behold thy sword, O Regin!" he laughed.

Then Regin forged another sword and said: "Surely thou wilt be content with this, though thou be hard to please in the matter of a weapon."

But again Sigurd struck upon the anvil, and again the sword fell to pieces. Then he turned wrathfully to Regin: "Art thou also a liar and a traitor like thy father and brother?"

And thus saying he went to his mother, and seating himself at her feet, he began: "Is it true, my mother, that Sigmund, my father, gave thee the Magic Sword of Odin in two pieces?"

"That is true enough," said she.

Then Sigurd entreated: "Give them then to me, I pray thee, for only in such wise shall I get a sword to my mind."

Then the queen knew that he looked to win great fame with that weapon, and she gave him the pieces; and he took them to Regin and bade him make a sword therefrom.

And though Regin's evil heart was wroth because of the words that the youth had spoken, he dared not refuse. So he set to work, and when he carried the finished sword from out the forge, it seemed to his helpers that fire burned along its edges.

"Take thy sword," said the old man, "and if this fails, I have lost my skill in sword-making."

This time when Sigurd smote upon the anvil the keen steel clove into the metal right up to the hilt, and he pulled it out unhurt. Then he went to the river and flung up-stream a tuft of wool, and when the tide carried the wool against the edge of the sword it was cut in two. And then was Sigurd satisfied and his heart rejoiced.

Upon his return Regin met him. "Now that I have made thee this good sword," said he, "wilt thou, for thy part, keep thy word, and go against Fafnir the dragon?"

"Surely will I do that thing," said Sigurd, "but first I must avenge my father."

So he went to the king, and bowing before him said: "Here have I now lived all my lifetime, and thanks and gratitude are owing from me to you, with all due honour. But now will I go hence to meet the sons of Hunding, that they may know that the

Volsungs are not all dead; and I would have your goodwill go with me upon the journey."

The king approved of Sigurd's spirit, and said he would give him whatsoever he desired; and therewith a great army was prepared, with ships and weapons, so that he might proceed on his journey in due state and power. And Sigurd himself steered the ship with the dragon's head, which was the finest of the fleet.

At first they ran before a fair wind; but after a few days there arose a great storm, and the sky and sea were red like blood. And as they sailed close along the shore, a certain men hailed them and asked who was captain of that array; and they told him that their chief was Sigurd, son of Sigmund, on his way to win fame for himself.

And the stranger said: "There is none like Sigurd, son of Sigmund, on this earth; so now, I pray thee, take me on board."

So they made for land and took the man aboard. Old he was and one-eyed; and his grey hat was slouched far over his face. And Sigurd saw that he was no ordinary traveller, and asked therefore if he could tell, before ever they reached land, what their fate would be on those stormy waters and in the battle that was to come.

Then said the Traveller: "Thou shalt land safe and sound, and victory shall be thine in the fight if thou shalt see these signs: First, a raven sitting on a tree; next, two warriors coming into the courtyard to meet thee, when the tramp of thy feet is heard; third, a wolf howling under boughs of ash. But see to it, that none of thy warriors look at the moon as she sets, nor trip up their feet as they march out to meet their foe. Let each warrior be well washed, well combed, and well fed—and if all these things come to pass, then have no fear as to who shall win the day."

Even as he spoke the wind abated, and the waves were stilled, and the ships were thenceforth wafted by friendly breezes to the shores of the realm of the sons of Hunding. But the instant they landed the mysterious stranger vanished, and by this Sigurd knew that once again he had been visited by All-Father Odin; and he went on his way rejoicing.

And as he passed up the strand a raven sitting upon a tree croaked at him; a short way farther on a wolf crouched howling under an ash; and as he approached the court of the king, the two sons of Hunding advanced from the courtyard to see what was meant by the tramp of armed men.

Now the news of the coming of the strangers soon spread far and wide over the land, and the people rose with one accord in defence of Lygni their king.

So he advanced upon Sigurd with a vast host, and an exceeding fierce fight began. Skulls were split, helmets shivered, and shields cut in two, full many times ere that day's work was done. Ever in the front of the fight rode Sigurd, with his good sword flashing, and wheresoever he went his foes fell back before him, for his like had never been seen by any man.

Then came against him the sons of Hunding, and Sigurd smote them down, one after the other, beginning with Lygni the king, until there were none left, and very few of their folk.

Then away sailed Sigurd, flushed with victory, to his mother and his stepfather, by whom he was received with much honour. But when he had been at home a little while, Regin came to him and said: "Perhaps now thou wilt have leisure to keep thy word and humble the crest of Fafnir to the earth, since thou hast avenged thy father and others of the Volsung kin."

And Sigurd answered: "That will I hold to, for I have pledged my word."

So it came to pass that Sigurd and Regin rode together to the heath where Fafnir dwelt; and they passed along the way by which the dragon was wont to creep down to the water to drink. So long was this terrible creature that he would lie crouched on a cliff sixty feet high when he drank of the water below. When Sigurd saw the huge tracks that he had made he said to Regin: "Sayest thou that this dragon is no greater than other such beasts? Methinks he leaves tracks behind him that are strangely well marked."

"There is naught to fear," said Regin. "Make thee a hole and sit down in it, and when the dragon comes to drink, smite him through the heart, and so shalt thou win for thyself great fame."

"But," said Sigurd, "what will happen when the burning blood of the dragon falls upon me?"

Now Regin well knew that no man could endure that frightful stream and live, and he wished to make an end of Sigurd when he had slain the beast. Therefore he answered wrathfully: "Of what use is it to give advice if thou art fearful of everything? Not like thy kin art thou, careless of perils."

With this undeserved taunt he rode away, for he himself was sore afraid, and dared not abide the coming of the dragon.

So Sigurd rode alone over the heath, and when he came to the marks where the tracks lay deep he began to dig a pit, as Regin had told him. But while he was busy at work an old man, wearing a big grey hat over his face, passed by and asked what he was doing. And when he had been told, he said:

"That was no wise advice that was given thee. Rather dig trenches in the midst of the dragon track, that the blood may run therein; and do thou then crouch in one of these and run thy sword through his heart as he drags his huge shape overhead."

And with these words he vanished.

Sigurd could not doubt the wisdom of this advice and he did as he had been bidden; and when he heard the dragon approaching he hid himself, his sword ready in his hand.

The roar of the dragon shook the earth for miles around, and Sigurd saw streams of venom issuing from his jaws as he drew near. But this did not affright him; he waited until the huge shape loomed overhead, and then thrust his sword, with all the strength he could command, as far as it would go into the loathsome breast.

Then followed a scene of violence beyond the power of words to express. A great roar, which shook the very heavens, went up from the cavernous throat, and well it was for Sigurd that he darted aside with the quickness of light. The huge coils unwound and contracted again in the monster's agony, and the furious lashing of his enormous tail utterly destroyed the surrounding vegetation, while his cruel talons, all powerless now to do aught else, ploughed deep furrows in the hard and rocky soil. All nature seemed to be undergoing its final convulsions in the few moments which elapsed ere the monster at length lay limp and gasping in the last throes of death.

Then, with the voice of Fafnir the dwarf, he asked in feeble accents: "Who art thou, and what is thy kin, that thou wast bold to lift weapon against me?"

And his foe made answer: "Sigurd am I called, of Volsung kin."

Then Fafnir asked: "Who urged thee to this deed, O bright-eyed boy?"

And Sigurd replied: "A bold heart urged me, and a strong hand and sharp sword aided me in the doing thereof."

But Fafnir's eyes were opened at the approach of death, and he said: "Regin, my brother, has brought about my end, and even now he is plotting to bring about thine also. Full soon shall the red gold of Andvari's hoard begin to work thy destruction. I give thee counsel, therefore, that thou ridest swiftly away without the gold; for often it happens that he who gets a death wound is none the less avenged."

But Sigurd answered: "I will not follow thy counsel, but even now will I rise to thy lair and take that great treasure which thou hast hoarded there."

And Fafnir answered: "Have thine own will. Yet shalt that gold be a curse to thee, and a curse to whosoever possesses it hereafter."

With this warning the loathsome creature breathed his last, and at the same moment the sun broke through the clouds, casting a glamour over the heath which only so lately had been the haunt of evil and a place of desolation.

Now, when it was plain that nothing more was to be feared from the dragon, came Regin from the place of safety where he lurked. And since he feared lest Sigurd should claim the treasure as his reward for slaying Fafnir, he began to accuse him of having murdered his kinsman, and to remind him that, according to the law of the Northmen, he could now require Sigurd's own life.

But Sigurd said: "I did but kill him at thy wish, O Regin, and with the good sword that thou thyself did make for me."

"Ah yes," said the traitor warily, "it was my good sword and not thy arm that has done the deed, and therefore no thanks are due to thee. But now will I count thee guiltless of my brother's blood if thou wilt cut out the heart of the dragon and give me to eat of it."

This Sigurd promised to do, and he made a fire and set about roasting the heart of the monster upon a rod. But presently, as he felt the heart to see if it were cooked enough, he burnt his fingers so severely that at once he set them in his mouth to soothe the smart. And the moment the heart-blood of Fafnir touched his tongue his ears were open to the voices of the birds, and he understood the meaning of their songs in the bushes hard by.

And this was what the woodpeckers sang, chuckling all the time: "There thou sittest, Sigurd, roasting the heart of Fafnir for another, whereas if thou ate it thyself thou wouldst become wisest of men."

And the swallows twittered: "See where lies Regin, who is in mind to kill the man who trusts in him."

And the raven croaked: "Let Sigurd then cut off his head and so have all the gold-hoard for his own."

And the eagle screamed: "Why did he not ride away with that hoard at once? Then might he have found the hill where Brunhild lies."

And the owl hooted: "Ay, let him now take his chance and slay the man who will surely kill him if he lets him live."

Then Sigurd arose, and he scrupled not to slay Regin; for he knew that he was about to betray him unto his death.

Then once more the birds began to sing. And this time they sang with glee of a warrior-maiden sleeping fast on a high mountain in the midst of a ring of glittering flames; and through this fiery ring only the bravest of heroes might pass and awake her from sleep.

> "On a mountain fell
> A warrior-maid fast sleeps
> Where a ring of flame
> Perfect safety keeps.
> None may take her hence
> Save a hero bold,
> For only at a hero's touch
> Will those fires burn cold."

Then was Sigurd fired with desire to find that fair maiden. So, after partaking of the dragon's heart, he leapt on his horse and rode along in the monster's tracks till he reached the place where, deep down in the earth, the gold lay hoarded. And there he found the store of treasure, which he placed in two great chests upon the back of his good horse, meaning to walk alongside. But the horse would not stir a foot until Sigurd, guessing what was in his mind, leapt upon his back; whereat Greyfell galloped away at once as though he were carrying no weight at all.

CHAPTER XIX

How Sigurd Won the Hand of Brunhild

*This is the tale the Northmen tell of how
Sigurd braved the flames, and what befell*

ON and on, over level plain, by wild marshes, through winding ways, galloped Greyfell, until at last he brought Sigurd to the foot of a mountain that is called Hindfell. And before him, on the crest of that height, he saw a great light as of a fire burning, so that the flames seemed to touch the sky.

Riding up the slope Sigurd found himself at length face to face with a ring of lurid fire, crackling and roaring with a noise like thunder. But without a moment's hesitation he plunged into the very midst of this.

Naught did he care for peril who had come to seek such prize, and, as if daunted by the courage of the Volsung, the fierce flames shrank back as he advanced, leaving ever a magic circle in which he rode unscathed, while all around they roared like some hungry lion robbed of its prey. They rose wave upon wave to the very sky, but their fierce glare shone with glory upon Sigurd, and his form was at that of the Sun-god when he rises from the everlasting hills at the dawn of day.

And suddenly, as though their work was done, the flames flickered and fell, leaving only a broad ring of pale ashes behind the hero as he rode on to where loomed the massive shape of a great castle hung with shields.

The doors of this castle stood wide open, and not a warrior was to be seen; so, dismounting, Sigurd entered the great hall, and at first saw no one—neither man, woman, nor child. But presently he came to a room where he saw a figure, clad all in armour, lying stretched upon a couch. Approaching thither, Sigurd removed the helmet, and saw, to his astonishment, the face of a beautiful maiden fast asleep. He called to her and tried to awaken her, but in vain. Then he cut off the breastplate, which was fastened so closely that it seemed as though it had grown into her flesh, and then the sleeves and the long steel boots; and at length she lay before him in her garments of fine white linen, over which fell long, thick tresses of golden hair. Sigurd bent over her in admiration, and at that moment she opened her beautiful eyes and gazed in wonder at his face. Then she arose, and looked with joy at the rising sun, but her gaze returned to Sigurd; and they two loved each other at first sight.

When they had communed tenderly together, Sigurd told who he was and whence he came; and Brunhild rejoiced to hear the tale. "For," said she, "none but a hero might pass through that ring of fire."

Then said Sigurd: "Tell me now, fair Brunhild, how thou camest to this lonely fire-girt castle."

And she told him this tale:

"A warrior-maiden am I—chief of those Valkyrs who carry off the valiant dead to the halls of Valhalla and ply them with mead at the banquet. But many years ago I gave dire offence to All-Father Odin, as thou shalt hear.

"Two kings had a quarrel, and determined to put their feud to the issue of the sword. One was named Helm Gunnar. He was an old man and a mighty warrior, and to him had Odin promised the victory.

"But for the other, young Agnar, my heart was filled with pity; and so I disregarded the command of Odin and struck down Helm Gunnar in the fight, the victory thus going to Agnar.

"Then did All-Father Odin, in his wrath, decree that I should be cast out from Valhalla and be banished to the earth, there to find a husband like any other maiden of Midgard. But I was sore afraid, for I feared to mate with a coward—I, who had been a warrior-maiden from my birth. And All-Father Odin was pitiful, and placed me in this castle on Hindfell, and surrounded me with a barrier of flames, through which none but a hero would dare to pass. But first he pierced me with the Thorn of Sleep, that I might not grow old in the years of waiting—that I should awake, as thou seest me, just as I was when I began to sleep, at the touch of a brave man."

Then Sigurd told her all his story, and when she knew that he was bound on adventurous quest she would not let him stay long by her side, but bade him go forth and win honour for himself and afterwards return to her again. Meantime she promised to await his return in the castle, protected by the ring of flames, which should be rekindled on his departure. "For none but Sigurd," said she, "will be brave enough to make his way through such flames as these, and so shall I be safe until thy return."

So Sigurd made ready to depart; but first he took Andvari's golden ring, and placing it upon Brunhild's finger, as they stood together on the mountain crest, he vowed to love none but her as long as his life should last.

CHAPTER XX

How the Curse of the Gold is Fulfilled

This is the tale the Northmen tell of how Sigurd was foully slain in the land of the Niblungs

Now when Sigurd had ridden far upon his way, he came to the land of the Niblungs, a place of eternal mists, ruled over by Giuki and his wife Grimhild. Three fine sons had they and one daughter, Gudrun, the fairest maiden upon earth.

But Grimhild was a witch-wife—a fierce-hearted woman, learned in magic and filled with crafty wile.

When they saw Sigurd riding into the courtyard with his glittering armour and his burden of treasure, the king and queen said to one another: "Surely one of the Asas has come hither; for the array of this stranger shines with the gold-gleam, and his horse is mightier than other horses, and the man himself excels in bearing all that we have ever seen."

So the king went out with his court to greet Sigurd, and asked: "Who art thou, who ridest into my kingdom without the leave of my sons, as none have dared to do before?"

And he answered: "Sigurd am I, the son of Sigmund."

And the king said: "Be thou welcome here then, and take from our hands whatsoever thou wilt have."

So for a time Sigurd lived in great honour at the court of the Niblungs, from whence he fared forth upon many adventures with the princes of that land, and ever was he foremost of them all.

During this time Brunhild was always in his memory, and he talked so often of her that at length the evil heart of Grimhild, the queen, was roused to jealousy. She bethought herself that, could he but be made to forget the maiden of the Flaming Castle, he might marry Gudrun, her daughter; and so all the wealth of Andvari's hoard might remain in the court of the Niblungs for ever. On a day, therefore, she mixed a magic potion, and gave it to Sigurd, saying:

"We have great joy in thy visit here, and would give thee the best that we enjoy. Now take this horn, and drink therefrom."

So he drank with gladness; and from that moment all remembrance of Brunhild was blotted from his mind, as though she had never been. And, as the queen had hoped, he began to look with eyes of affection upon Gudrun, the fair maiden whom he saw every day, so that the Niblung princes, who had grown to love and honour Sigurd more and more, came to him and said: "Great good thou hast brought us, Sigurd, and exceeding strength thou givest to our realm. We pray thee therefore to abide with us for ever, and thou shalt have rule in our land, and we will give thee our sister in marriage, whom another man would not get for all his prayers." Then the heart of the Volsung responded, and they swore brotherhood together, even as if they were children of one father and mother; and in due time Gudrun was married to Sigurd with all joy and festivity.

Yet, in the midst of all this glee, a strange feeling oppressed the heart of Sigurd. Some old memory seemed to be striving within him, but, try as he would, he could not give it definite shape.

Time passed and King Giuki died, Gunnar, his son, succeeding him. And as he had no wife, his mother, Grimhild, said: "Fair is thy life and fortune, O my son, but one thing thou lackest. Go, seek for thyself a wife who shall be a joy to thy house."

"But where can I find one who will be a worthy queen of the Niblungs?" asked Gunnar.

And his mother answered: "Fair among the daughters of the earth and bravest of warrior-maidens is Brunhild. In her Castle of Flames she awaits the bridegroom who shall dare to penetrate the barrier of fire. Go then, seek her out, and Sigurd will ride with thee."

So Gunnar and Sigurd arrayed themselves joyously and rode away, till on the crest of a high mountain they saw a castle with a golden roof and all about it a ring of flaming fire.

Then right eagerly they pricked their steeds, but all too long it seemed ere they gained the summit. At length they reached the fiery wall, and Gunnar put his tired horse at it without pause. But the horse trembled and stood stock still. Again and again he tried him, but always with the same result, until, at length, Gunnar cried to Sigurd: "Lend me thy steed, Sigurd, for mine will not brave this fire."

"With all my heart," replied Sigurd, leaping off Greyfell. But when Gunnar had mounted the horse, Greyfell would not stir, and he too trembled before the flames.

Then Gunnar sprang to earth, and stamped with impatience, for he thought it shame to go afoot into the presence of the maid. Presently he remembered that his witch-mother had given him a magic potion which would enable a man to take the face and form of another at will. So he proposed that Sigurd should take his appearance and win Brunhild for him by proxy, for he knew that Greyfell would dare anything with his beloved master astride his back.

Remembering naught, Sigurd eagerly accepted the mission, and when he had drunk of the potion prepared by Gunnar he leaped again upon the back of Greyfell, who sprang at once into the heart of the fire.

Then the flames roared with a thunderous sound, and shot up high into the sky; but next moment they died away into a heap of grey ashes, and Sigurd, unharmed, entered the hall where Brunhild sat and waited for her faithless lover.

As he entered she started up with a cry of joy, which quickly died away when, in place of Sigurd's fair hair and bright blue eyes, she saw the dark locks and flashing black eyes of Gunnar.

"What man art thou?" she asked.

"Gunnar am I called," said Sigurd, "and through the flames have I ridden to woo thee for my bride."

But she looked sadly at the floor and said: "Methought none but Sigurd the Volsung could have dared those awful flames."

Then Sigurd thought to entice the maiden. "Much gold shall be thine," said he, "if thou wilt marry Gunnar the Niblung."

But she said: "Talk not to me of gold. All-Father Odin promised me a hero-husband, and I, a warrior-maiden, will marry no silken knight for gold."

Now Brunhild had bound herself by a solemn pledge to marry him who should ride through the fire, so in the end she was obliged to submit to her wooer's will; wherefore she took off the ring from Andvari's hoard that Sigurd had placed upon her finger, and gave it to him, with her promise to appear at the court of the Niblungs in ten days' time. Sigurd gave her another ring in exchange, and then rejoined Gunnar, with whom he rode back home, after having taken back his own form and likeness.

And only to Gudrun, his wife, did Sigurd reveal the secret of how Brunhild had been won for her brother Gunnar, and to her he gave the ring from Andvari's hoard which she had returned to him.

Now, when ten days had passed by, Brunhild came to the land of the Niblungs, and was met in solemn state by Gunnar at the door of his palace. Then was held high festival at the marriage celebration, after which Gunnar led his bride into the great hall where Sigurd and Gudrun sat side by side upon the high daïs. When Brunhild saw her old lover she trembled violently and her face went ashy pale, then her beautiful eyes met Sigurd's with a look of such intense sadness and meaning that the spell was dissolved, and the remembrance of the love he had given her rushed suddenly back into his mind, well-nigh overwhelming him with grief.

Yet was he bound to Gudrun, as Brunhild was to Gunnar, so no more passed at that time.

Now one day, when the birds sang pleasantly and all nature rejoiced in the warmth of the summer sun, the two princesses, Gudrun and Brunhild, went down to the river to bathe; and Gudrun waded the farther into the water, saying scornfully that thus it became the wife to do whose husband was the bravest in the world.

Then the bitter feelings which for long had vexed the soul of Brunhild would not be restrained, and they poured forth in a torrent of wrath like some mighty waters when the dam gives way before its constant force.

Gudrun retorted upon her by telling how that it was Sigurd, not Gunnar, who had braved the fiery flames, and in proof of this she showed in triumph the ring from Andvari's hoard which she wore upon her finger.

Now when she heard this, Brunhild was beside herself with rage that she should have been thus tricked, and she went to her husband and said: "Never again shalt thou see me glad in thy hall, nor hear me speak words of peace and gladness within thy borders, for thou hast deceived me, and art no hero as I thought."

And for many days after that Brunhild neither ate nor drank, but set wide the doors of her bower and lamented, so that all folk heard and marvelled.

In vain they tried to comfort her; she would not hear even the soothing words of Sigurd, whom Gudrun had sent to her, saying scornfully, however, as he went: "Give her red gold, forsooth, and smother up her grief and anger therewith."

At length Brunhild sent for her husband, and bade him put Sigurd to death, saying that she had vowed to marry the man who should come to her through the fire, and, since this was now impossible, Sigurd must surely die, that she might be released from her oath.

And at that Gunnar was sorely troubled, for he loved Sigurd very dearly. But he said to himself: "Brunhild is better to me than all things else, and the fairest of all women, and I will lay down my life rather than lose her love."

So he sent for his brother and told him that he had made up his mind to kill Sigurd. And Högni, his brother, was very loth, and declared that such an act of treachery would bring great shame upon the land. But Gunnar reminded him of the gold-hoard, and of how all would be theirs if Sigurd were out of the way. And at length they determined to incite their younger brother, Guttorm, to do the deed.

But Guttorm, in his turn, was unwilling until they mixed for him a magic drink, which made him fierce and wild and eager for bloodshed, so that he was ready for whatever might befall.

At midnight, therefore, Guttorm crept, sword in hand, to Sigurd's chamber; but, as he bent over his pillow, he saw the bright blue eyes of the young hero fixed steadily upon him; and he fled, for so keen and eager were the eyes of Sigurd that few might look upon him. A second time he went in, and again the same thing happened.

But the third time Sigurd lay asleep; then Guttorm took his sword and drove it through his breast.

Wounded to death, the young man had just strength to raise himself, seize his good sword and hurl it after Guttorm as he fled, and the magic weapon cut him in two ere he reached the door. Then Sigurd fell back into the arms of Gudrun and died.

Then did great grief fall upon the land of the Niblungs; and a mighty funeral pyre was built for Sigurd, and his body was laid thereon.

Gudrun, his wife, sat silent and apart, her heart breaking for her hero-husband; but Brunhild, when she saw what she had done, was filled with grief and despair beyond endurance, and snatching a dagger from her handmaidens, she stabbed herself and so died.

In such wise had the doom of the Magic Gold descended upon Regin and Fafnir, and upon Sigurd and Brunhild. Nor was this the end of the misery it was to work.

Loathing the thought of life in her brother's palace, Gudrun now fled to the court of Alf, the foster-father of Sigurd, where for some years she remained, busying herself in working a vast piece of tapestry on which she embroidered the heroic deeds of Sigurd.

But after a time Atli, King of the Huns, the brother of Brunhild, sent to Gunnar to demand that compensation should be made to him for his sister's death; and to him Gunnar promised that, in satisfaction for this, he should receive the hand of his sister Gudrun in marriage. So the Niblung princes sent and fetched her from the court of Alf, and forced her to marry Atli, much against her will.

Now at Atli's court her talk was ever of Sigurd and of the wondrous gold-hoard he had brought to the Niblungs' land. And so it came to pass that the greed of Atli was kindled when he heard of that treasure, and he determined to make it his own.

So he sent a messenger to invite all the Niblung princes to visit his court, intending, when he had them in his power, to put an end to them. Now Gudrun guessed what was in Atli's mind, and therefore she took off the gold ring from Andvari's hoard, and twined about it a wolf's hair as a sign of warning; and this she sent by the same messenger to her brothers.

But this messenger untwined the wolf's hair and gave only the ring to Gunnar, who took it as a signal of good faith and gladly accepted the invitation.

Högni alone was unwilling to accept the invitation, but when he found that Gunnar would pay no heed to him, he prepared to go along with him.

First, however, he persuaded his brother to take that great treasure-hoard and to cast it into a deep hole at the bottom of a mighty river, where none might find it save themselves.

So Gunnar agreed, and Högni took the gold, and, standing on a great rock in the midst of the river, he flung it, with a huge splash, into the water.

"Down then and whirling outward the ruddy gold fell forth,
  As a flame in the dim grey morning flashed out a kingdom's worth;
  Then the waters roared above it, the wan water and the foam
  Flew up o'er the face of the rock-wall as the tinkling gold fell home,
  Unheard, unseen, forever, a wonder and a tale,
  Till the last of earthly singers from the sons of men shall fail."

Not yet, however, had the curse of that gold-hoard been entirely fulfilled. For when the brave Niblungs reached the hall of Atli, they found no welcome awaiting them, but sharp swords and hostile looks. Fiercely they fought, but to no avail, and at length all were slain save only Gunnar and Högni.

Then Atli had each brought before him in turn, fast bound as they were, and promised to give freedom to him who would first reveal to him the hiding-place of the gold-hoard. But they laughed in contempt, even when they were put to the torture in his presence.

Then Högni, being weary of his life in chains, made an agreement with Gunnar, so that when next King Atli asked the latter to tell him the secret, he replied that he had made an oath not to reveal the hiding-place while Högni lived, but that when he saw his brother was dead, he would do all that Atli bade him. So they killed Högni, and the Battle Maidens carried him away to the joys of Valhalla. But when they showed proofs of his death to his brother, and bade him tell the whereabouts of the hoard, Gunnar laughed a proud laugh and declared that now the secret rested with him alone, and it should never be revealed.

So, in his fury of disappointment, the king ordered him to be thrown, with chained hands, into a den full of poisonous serpents; and his harp was flung in after him. Then did Gunnar sit smiling in their midst, and played with his toes upon the instrument until all the creatures, save one, were fast asleep.

But this one serpent, whom men say was the witch-mother of Atli in disguise, bit Gunnar in the side, and thus died the last of the Niblungs.

Of that race Gudrun still remained, and she now planned a thing which should avenge the blood of her kinsmen and end her own unhappy life.

So she took the sword of Sigurd, which Gunnar had given into her hands, and slew Atli and placed him dead upon a ship. And when she had cast it adrift, she flung herself into the sea; and so died.

Thus did Andvari's hoard fulfil the curse that had been set upon all those who should be concerned with it. But the glittering treasure itself lies hidden far beneath the waves of the mighty river Rhine, and only the water-sprites know where it is hid.

CHAPTER XXI

The Boyhood of Frithiof the Bold

*This is the tale the Northmen tell of how Frithiof
the Bold asked for the hand of Ingeborg the Fair*

ONCE upon a time there lived in Norway a king named Bele, who had three children. Helge and Halfdan were his sons, and his daughter was called by the name of Ingeborg.

Now Ingeborg was the fairest of maidens, and had moreover

such a fine wit and understanding that all men said she was the first and best of the good king's children.

To the west of the settlement in which King Bele lived rose up a great white temple, hedged around with a lofty wall of wood. This temple was sacred to Balder the Beautiful; and so much did men honour him in those days of old, that they made strict laws that within the enclosure in which his temple stood no man should hold converse with a woman, nor should any harm be done to man or beast.

On the other side of the inlet on which stood the abode of Bele was a village ruled by a mighty man of valour named Thorsten. This Thorsten had a son called Frithiof, who at the time of his birth was bigger and stronger than all other babes, and grew up not only tall but also bold and brave of heart; so that men named him Frithiof the Bold.

Now Thorsten was a sea-rover. So he sent his little son to a sturdy yeoman called Hilding, that he might be brought up by him and taught all that a Viking ought to know. For the education of a Viking was no small thing. He might not claim the title till he had lifted the mighty stone that stood before the door of the king and had borne it across the pathway. And he had to learn what was meant by the "triple oath"—that he would not capture woman or child in battle, nor seek refuge in a tempest, nor wait to bind up his wounds before the fight was spent.

Now it so happened that, while the children of the king were still young, their mother died, and the little princess was also placed in the care of Hilding and his wife. Thus Frithiof and Ingeborg grew up together, and were more beautiful and brave and clever than all the other boys and girls of that place.

Thorsten, Frithiof's father, was the king's right hand, and now that Bele was grown old and feeble he managed most of the affairs of the kingdom. And Frithiof too was useful to the king, more so, indeed, than were his own two sons.

Thorsten had a famous swift ship, called *Ellida,* which was rowed by fifteen men on each side, and each oar required the strength of two men to pull it; but Frithiof was so strong that he would row two oars at once.

The king's two sons, Helge and Halfden, differed much from each other in their appearance and characters, but they were

alike in their jealous dispositions. In particular they grudged
Frithiof his growing renown, and hated him in their hearts for
his great strength, which far exceeded theirs.

At length King Bele fell very sick, and, knowing that he was
about to die, he sent for Thorsten and their three sons and said:

"I trow that this sickness will be to my death, and I have called
you, my children, to hear the last counsel of your father.

"My sons, govern the realm in peace, and let force stand sen-
tinel at the borders. The king is helpless who hath not the con-
fidence and affection of his people, and the throne is insecure if
it rest not on a foundation of just and equal laws.

"Choose not the forward for your counsellors, but confide,
rather, in the wisdom and valour of one tried friend. Thorsten
and I have faithfully kept friendship's troth in steadfast union, so
do ye, in weal or woe, wend together with Frithiof. If ye three
will hold together as one man, your match shall not be seen
through all our Northland.

"Let my last words be for my beloved Ingeborg. She hath
grown lovely in peace as the rose. Helge, be thou her guardian,
and let no storm-wind scatter those fair petals."

Then Thorsten, in his turn, addressed Frithiof:

"My son, I too must shortly wend to Valhalla, and I rejoice to
think that Odin has bestowed upon thee much strength and
courage of heart. It is good, but remember that strength without wit is soon brought to naught, even as the bear, who wields
in his paw the strength of twelve men, is laid low by a thrust
from the sword of one. Beware of arrogance, which goes before
a fall, and bend before the will of the king's sons. Above all, will
noble deeds and do thou every right."

After this the old men gave directions for their burial, and
they charged their sons to lay them beneath two barrows or
mounds, one on each side of the narrow firth, whose murmurs
would ever be sweet music as they slept, and across whose
waves their spirits would hold converse as of yore.

After the death of Thorsten, Frithiof took his land and
ruled in his stead, with the aid of his two foster-brothers,
Björn and Osmund. And he was now the owner of *Ellida*, the
good ship which understood every word that was spoken to
her, as though she were alive; and of two other heirlooms of

priceless value. The first was a sword, Angurvadel it was named, which tradition said had been forged in Eastern lands by the dwarfs. Its hilt was of hammered gold, and the blade was covered with magic runes, which in peace were dull, but which flamed blood-red when the sword was brandished in war. The other was a marvellous arm-ring, carved with all the wonders of the heavens.

It had always been the custom of the House of Thorsten to invite the household of the king each year to a banquet, and so, soon after he had succeeded to his father's place, Frithiof gave a feast more magnificent than any that had been given hitherto. For he knew that, with her two brothers, would come also Ingeborg the Fair, whom he loved with his whole heart. And while the two young kings sat at the board with hostile looks and downcast faces, this sweet princess laughed among her maidens like a sunny day in June. Her hair was as golden as the buttercups in the spring meadows, her eyes were blue like a summer sea, and her face fair as a hawthorn bush when it first opens its buds of red and white.

But Frithiof was silent in her presence, for he had no words save "I love thee" in his mind.

After this festival, the two kings turned home again in deeper wrath than ever, for they saw how all men loved Frithiof and had him in honour.

But after their departure, Frithiof grew silent and sad of countenance, and when his foster-brother Björn questioned him as to the cause he answered: "Sad am I because I love the Princess Ingeborg with all my heart, and now would I ask for her in marriage. But I am not of royal birth, and much I fear that my suit will be refused."

"Let us at least make trial," said practical Björn; and so, together with a band of followers, they set off in the swift dragon-ship *Ellida* to the strand where, upon their father's burial mound, the kings sat in judgment with their people.

Then Frithiof stood forth and in manly words made his request for the hand of Ingeborg the Fair. But the kings said scornfully:

"Think not that we would give our sister to a peasant's son.

She is for a proud Northland chieftain, not for such as you, though all men may boast of your wondrous deeds."

"Then," said Frithiof, in slow-gathering wrath, "my errand is soon finished. Remember, that if this is your final answer, I will never give you help in trouble, however much you may require it."

"Our kingdom requires not your service," they answered jeeringly, "we can protect it ourselves. But if you need employment, why, we can give you a servant's place among our household men."

Then Frithiof reared his great head, saying proudly:

"No man of yours am I, but, as my father was, I am a man for myself. And now, were it not for the honour I bear to our fathers' graves, your words would cost you dear. Hereafter come not within range of my sword."

And as he spoke, with one blow he cleft the golden war shield of Helge with his good sword, and the two halves fell clashing to the ground.

Chapter XXII

Frithiof and Ingeborg

This is the tale the Northmen tell of how
Ingeborg went to dwell in Balder's grove

FAR in the south of that land lived a mighty ruler, whose name was Ring. Wise was he, and king of a land like the groves of the gods, where the corn crops waved each year and peace and justice flourished within its borders. For thirty years had he ruled his kingdom, and each year his people rose up and called him blessed.

Now one day this king sat deep in thought upon his golden chair, and when he at length pushed it back from the board, his chieftains rose up gladly to hear his words.

And the king said: "It is now a weary while since the queen, my wife, left me sorrowful upon the earth and went to dwell in the bowers of the blessed ones in Asgard. Never again shall I find a queen so good and fair; but my children cry to me for a mother's care and I must seek another wife for their sake.

"Now it comes to my remembrance that often King Bele visited my hall, and with him sometimes came his fair daughter Ingeborg. 'Tis on her my choice shall fall, for though I am old and she is but a young girl, I know that she will be a good mother to my children.

"Take therefore gold and gems from yon oak presses, and let the minstrels tune their harps and go forth to ask her in marriage from the sons of Bele."

So a long line of harpers went forth, followed by youths in glad array, and they stood before King Helge and King Halfdan, and gave to them the message of King Ring.

Now Helge was nothing loth to give his fair sister to the king, although he was an old man and she but a young girl; but, since he was always very heedful of the will of the gods, he offered sacrifice and carefully consulted the wise men and the wise women and all the omens as to whether this thing should be. And all with one consent answered that the marriage must not be allowed.

So Helge refused the king's request courteously enough, saying that man must obey when the gods decree; but Halfdan, being rude and waggish of tongue, said: "King Greybeard himself should have ridden hither for his bride if he is not too old to mount his horse!"

Then the messenger returned wrathful, and King Ring said grimly: "They shall soon see if King Greybeard be too old to take revenge," and with that he struck his war shield, as it hung on the tree above him, such a blow that the echo of it was borne even to the hall of Helge and Halfdan. Then he sent messengers, this time in warlike array, to the two kings, bidding them submit to his authority and pay him tribute. "If ye refuse," said they, "our king will send a great army and take the kingdom and utterly destroy you and your people."

But Helge and Halfdan answered with spirit:

"Not in our young days will we learn to do that which we will never know when old, and that is how to do shameful service to a neighbour king."

Then they summoned Hilding, their foster-father, and bade him go to Frithiof and pray him to come with his followers to their aid. And meantime, being in fear for their sister's safety, they sent her away to the dim grove where Balder's temple rose grey among the shadows. There, day by day, fair Ingeborg sat among her maidens at her embroidery, and as she drew the thread it was wet with her tears.

Now when Hilding, that good old yeoman, reached the hall of Frithiof, he found the hero sitting with Björn at a game of chess. Gladly was he greeted by the young man, who pointed to the High Chair, the chief seat at the board, and bade him sit and drink a horn of mead while they finished their game.

But Hilding, full of his errand, began at once to speak: "I am sent by the sons of Bele," said he. "They now salute thee and pray that thou wouldst go up to their help to battle against King Ring, who is about to attack their land with violence."

But Frithiof seemingly paid no heed to his words, saying only to his opponent: "Björn, thy king is in danger, beware! Yet a pawn can recover him even now."

Then Hilding urged: "Frithiof, my son, anger not the kings. Remember that they too have power, and that they threaten thee with a terrible fate if thou wilt not go forth to their aid."

But Frithiof only said to Björn:
"See how thou threatenest my castle in vain!"

"Grim and high the fierce wall rises,
Bright the Shield-tower shines within."

Then Hilding tried another argument.
"Son!" he cried, "knowest thou not how Ingeborg weeps all day within the Place of Balder? Wilt thou not fight for her release? Wilt thou leave her blue eyes to melt in vain?"

But Frithiof answered Björn, as though unheeding: "Björn, 'tis in vain thou tryest to take my queen, ever so dear and true to me. She is my favourite piece in all the game, and, come what will, I'll save my queen."

"What!" cried the old man. "Must I go forth unheeded, without even a reply, because of this child's game?"

Then Frithiof rose and pressed his hand kindly, saying: "Father, naught will make me change my mind, and what thou hast heard me say here in this place, thou mayest tell again to those who sent thee."

When the kings received the report of Hilding concerning Frithiof, they waited but to see that their sister Ingeborg was safe within the walls of Balder's grove, and then prepared to march with all the forces they could muster to meet King Ring.

Meantime Frithiof attired himself in his richest dress, and placed his golden ring upon his arm, and called on Björn and his servants to follow him.

"Whither now do we go, my brother?" asked Björn.

"To the grove of Balder," answered Frithiof shortly.

"That is not well," said Björn anxiously. "It will draw down the anger of the gods upon us."

"That remains to be seen," replied Frithiof.

So they rowed over the firth and entered Balder's grove, and made their way into Ingeborg's bower.

Now when she saw Frithiof, the blue eyes of Ingeborg flashed with joy, but she said gravely, as she rose to receive him: "Now wherefore art thou so bold, Frithiof, to come hither against the will of my brothers and to bring the wrath of the gods upon us?"

But Frithiof replied: "Nay, love, no perils attend us. Fear not the wrath of Balder; that gentle god will not punish true lovers. Let us kneel at his shrine. No incense is more grateful to his soul than the faith of two young hearts vowing eternal love."

So when they had knelt for a space they sat down side by side, and Frithiof drew the ring from off his arm and gave it to Ingeborg, saying: "This ring will I give thee if thou wilt promise never to part with it, but to send it to me when thou no longer hast need of it. And with it I plight thee my troth."

And in the same manner did Ingeborg give her own ring to Frithiof.

And then Ingeborg with fond entreaties implored her lover to seek Helge once again, and offer his hand, lest haply he might be reconciled. Long did Frithiof hesitate, but at last the melting eyes of Ingeborg could be denied no longer, and he promised that once again would he seek the kings in peace and friendship.

CHAPTER XXIII

Frithiof Braves the Storm

*This is the tale the Northmen tell of how Frithiof
the Bold went on a perilous adventure*

NOW when the two young kings met with Ring, and found that his forces were far stronger than theirs, their hearts failed them and they sent messengers to sue for peace. And it was arranged that they should submit to King Ring, and should give Ingeborg their sister to him in marriage, together with the third part of all their possession.

Now one morning tidings were brought to Frithiof by Björn, who cried: "The kings are returned home, and short enough will be our time of peace, for we have broken the law of Balder, and we shall have to pay."

But Frithiof, who knew no fear, bade him be at rest, saying that directly the kings had taken their seat upon their father's grave-mound, to hear the suits brought before them, he intended once again to claim the hand of Ingeborg.

So on the day appointed he sought the place where Helge sat, black as a thunder-cloud, with his warriors around him, and foolish Halfdan, jesting as usual, and playing with his sword, stood by his side. And Frithiof stood forth and said: "Not yet is thy kingdom free, O Helge, from the threat of battle. Give me then thy sister and my strong right arm shall fight for thee. Come, let this grudge between us be forgotten, for I am loth to bear myself ill towards the brother of Ingeborg and the sons of Bele. Here is my hand; but by the gods I swear that, if thou refuse, it shall never be stretched forth to thee in peace again."

At these words a shout broke from the listening throng and the air was rent with the noise of clashing weapons.

"Ay! Give him Ingeborg, for what swordsman in our land is like to him?"

And even foolish Halfdan joined in the prayer.

But Helge, still cold and hard, made reply:

"The peasant's son might indeed have claimed the Princess Ingeborg, but not he who has broken Balder's peace. Say, Frithiof, hast thou not spurned the law of Balder's house and spoken to my sister within his sacred walls?"

Then from the crowd of warriors came the murmur: "Say but nay, say nay! The word of Thorsten's son is good as any king's. Say nay! Say nay!"

But Frithiof made reply: "I will not lie to gain the joys of Asgard. I have seen thy sister and spoken to her within yon walls, yet have I not disturbed Balder nor broken his good peace."

Then all that assembly was filled with horror as they heard his words, for they all feared the wrath of the god. Hoarse and gloomy was the voice of Helge as he said:

"Now, by my great father's laws, I could condemn thee to banishment or death, but, even as great Balder was mild, so shall my judgment be.

"Far away on the isles of the west dwells a mighty jarl named Angantyr, who in my father's days paid yearly tribute to our land, and since his death has kept all back. Away then to his realm, collect the money, and bring it back to us. 'Tis said he is hardhanded, and will meet with the sharp sword him who asks for his gold, but what is that to thee? Hence, Frithiof, or be branded coward for evermore."

Then Frithiof bowed his head and departed, for he knew that it was the will of Balder that this thing should be.

But first he went again to visit his betrothed and to bid her a sad farewell. Heavy of heart was Ingeborg, for she knew that her brother had planned an expedition that should cost Frithiof his life; but Frithiof cheered her, reminding her that this Angantyr, whom men so dreaded, was his father's oldest friend.

So Frithiof prepared to set out on his journey, but first he made a pact with Helge that his possessions should rest in peace during his absence, and the promise was confirmed with oaths.

Then Frithiof set out with eighteen of his companions, and they went on board the swift ship *Ellida* and sailed out beyond the bay.

But no sooner had he departed than the kings plundered and burnt his village. After this, they sent two witches, and bade them send such a terrible tempest against Frithiof and his followers that they should all perish in the sea. To this the evil hags readily agreed, and, having climbed to the top of a high mountain, began to cast their wicked spells upon the winds.

Thus it came to pass that when Frithiof and his men had left the land far behind them there arose a great storm, and a mighty wind, which lashed the waves to the very stars and drove the ship violently along.

But Frithiof only smiled and sang:

> "Run, good ship, before the wind,
> Ingeborg thou soon shalt find.
> Ingeborg, the maid I love,
> Waits for me in Balder's grove."

Then said Björn, in fear and wrath: "Well would it be if thou hadst something better to do than to sing of Balder's grove."

But Frithiof laughed aloud, and showed him how the north wind was blowing them straight to the Solundar Isles, where they might find safe harbour. They did not bide there long, however, for the weather suddenly became calmer, and for awhile they sailed along before a favourable breeze. Then the wind began to freshen again, and when they were far out at sea a still mightier tempest arose, with so much sleet and snow that they could not see the prow of the vessel from the stern. The waves also beat over the ship, so that they had to bale incessantly. But Frithiof, though he toiled harder than them all, continued to laugh and sing, though Björn growled: "He who wanders far meets many a hindrance."

Then a great sea swept over the boat and nearly swamped her; and Frithiof cried: "See how the Swan Maidens are pledging us!" and set to work to bale with a good heart.

Still higher rose the storm, till the waves, like snow mountains, reared themselves above the ship; and Björn cried in despair: "Sure woe is now at hand, my foster-brother. Why didst thou ever enter the bower of Balder's grove?"

But Frithiof said with a laugh: "Methinks some of our good fellows will have to journey to the realms of Ran, the Sea-goddess, and we shall cut but a sorry figure there unless we go with a brave face and red gold in our hands."

So saying he took the gold ring that Ingeborg had given him and cut it in pieces and divided it among his men.

At last the storm grew still and the waves calm; but the ship was water-logged, and Frithiof called loudly on the men to bale her out.

"It is useless to try to do it," said the faint-hearted Björn, but Frithiof cried: "Come, brother, never despair, for it hath ever been a hero's custom to give what help he can as long as possible, come what may hereafter."

So they baled *Ellida* clear, and, seeing his companions were now worn out with toil, Frithiof bade them lie down in the boat and rest. And he himself took two oars at the prow and rowed onwards with his mighty strength til they came to land; and finding that his followers were still weak and weary he carried them over the surf on his shoulders and set them safely on shore.

Now the island on which they had landed was part of the domain of that Jarl Angantyr, and soon a message him:

"Tidings, my jarl. Men have come ashore, but they seem weary and helpless enough. Yet one of hem is so strong and fresh that he carries all the others to land."

"Surely," said the jarl, "that man must be Frithiof, son of my old friend Thorsten, a man renowned for all good deeds."

Then Angantyr sent messengers to bid Frithiof welcome and to bring him to his hall. And he prevailed upon his guest to pass the winter with him, and showed high hospitality to him and to all his men. But when Frithiof spoke of the errand on which he had come, the jarl said proudly: "No tribute shall King Helge have of me, but thou, my friend, shalt take back such treasure as thou wilt, and tribute thou mayest call it, or any other name, as thou desirest. For now it is clear to me that Helge hath laid a trap for thee, and such kings are but ill-esteemed in this land."

CHAPTER XXIV

Balder Forgives

*This is the tale the Northmen tell of how Frithiof
the Bold was wedded to Ingeborg the Fair*

Now while Frithiof was absent in the Western Isles there came Ring, that good old chieftain, northward to the land of the two young rulers, Helge and Halfdan.

Sorely grieved was Ingeborg when she knew that she must wed the stranger king, but she knew naught of what had happened to Frithiof, and was obliged to obey her brothers' will.

And as they sat at the marriage feast, Ring saw the bracelet upon her arm and knew that it had been Frithiof's; and he bade her take it off and give it to the wife of Helge that she might give it to the wanderer on his return.

In the following spring came Frithiof back again to Norway, having parted from Angantyr with much love and goodwill. But as he neared his home, one met him whom he knew, who said: "Black have grown th buildings here, and traces there are none of the hands of friends."

Then Frithiof held counsel with his men and they shaped their course to the hall of the kings. But upon arrival there he heard that they were away at Balder's grove offering a sacrifice. So he set off thither with Björn, leaving the rest with orders to make holes in all th ships, both large and small, that lay in that harbour. When they came to the entrance of the temple, Frithiof bade Björn stay outside and, entering alone, stood silent in the shadows watching where King Helge stood, crowned, by the altar of fire, whose flickering flames painted the great wooden image of Balder with a golden glory. Around the walls were ranged the ancient priests, silver-bearded, some with burning brands and others with flint knives for the sacrifice.

Up to King Helge then strode Frithiof and, taking from his girdle the bag of silver which he had received from Angantyr, he flung it in the face of the king, saying: "Receive thy tribute thus!" And so hard did he fling the money that it struck out two of Helge's teeth, and he fell senseless on the floor.

Now there were few but old men in the temple hall, and they were awed by the sight of Frithiof's gleaming blade.

So for a time he stood unmolested, but as he turned to go the arm-ring he had given to Ingeborg caught his eye, for it had been placed upon Balder's arm. "Pardon, O Balder," he said, "but thou wilt no claim a stolen jewel!" As he spoke he tugged at the ring, but it seemed to have grown fast to the wooden arm. Frithiof put forth all his strength, and suddenly the ring came away, but the great figure of the god fell prone across the altar, whose flames immediately enveloped it and lept up as though in triumph to the rafters of the hall.

Then was there great confusion as the flames spread rapidly. Frithiof stayed to render what aid was possible, but when it was seen that the temple was doomed to utter destruction he turned grief-stricken away, an rejoining his companions they put out to sea.

When King Helge came to his senses again his first thought was vengeance, and he summoned his men to pursue after Frithiof. But his ships had barely got under way when they began to sink, so that they had to put back quickly into harbour. Then in his fury did Helge snatch his bow to shoot an arrow after Frithiof, but so strongly did he pull it that the string broke and the bow fell useless from his hand.

Meantime, Frithiof sailed merrily out to sea; and when Björn questioned him as to what he meant to do next he replied: "Since I may no longer stay in Norway, I will learn the customs of the sea-chief, and will rove as a Viking."

So all through the summer they sailed to distant islands and far-off countries, winning both goods and renown, until he had become exceeding rich and famous. Wicked and cruel men he slew, but peasants and merchants and women he let go free, like the good Viking that he was.

At length, after four years had thus passed away, Frithiof said to Björn: "Weary am I of these expeditions, and therefore will I sail away to Uplands and hold discourse with good King Ring."

"It is not good," said Björn, "to trust thyself in a rival's power. If thou must do this rash thing at least go not alone."

"I am never alone," replied the hero, "while my sword hangs at my side."

Frithiof now made preparation for his journey, and when he said farewell to his companions he was clad in a cloak of skin which completely covered him, and he walked with two staves as one who is bowed down with years. His face, too, was covered with a great beard.

It was eventide when he entered the king's hall and stood far down by the door with his cloak drawn over his face.

Then the king said to the queen as she sat by him at table: "There has just come a man into the hall taller by far than other men."

And she answered without interest that that was no great news.

Then the king sent for the stranger and questioned him as to whence he came; and because he loved to show hospitality he bade him seat himself at his side. "But," said he, "let fall that shaggy hide, which covers, as I think, a proper man."

Then Frithiof showed himself in a dark-blue kirtle, with the ring gleaming on his arm and his sword girt to a broad silver belt, from which hung a well-filled purse. And when the queen saw that arm-ring she knew Frithiof, in spite of the great beard that he had grown; but she betrayed her recognition only by her changing colour and the heaving of her breast.

Now the king soon grew to love Frithiof, whom he compelled to stay with him all the winter through. Little and seldom spoke the queen to him, but by the king he was ever regarded with a glad and smiling countenance.

Then it came to pass that one day Frithiof had accompanied them to a banquet, and their way lay over a lake. And Frithiof warned the king that the ice on this lake was not safe. Scarcely had the king thanked him for his care when the ice broke, and the sledge with the royal pair upon it must have been submerged had not Frithiof dragged it forth and saved their lives. Then said the king, looking at him very kindly: "Well done, good friend, Frithiof the Bold cold not have done better had he been here."

The winter passed away, and one day, when the woods were full of green leaves, the king went forth into them with Frithiof as his only companion. Presently said the king: "Heavy am I with sleep, and here must I rest."

But Frithiof said: "Not so; let my lord journey home, for here is danger to those who sleep in the open air."

"I care not," said the king, and so laid himself down to sleep.

And as he slept Frithiof came and looked on him, and then quickly took his sword from its scabbard and flung it away.

Then the king opened his eyes and said: "Well hast thou resisted that temptation, Frithiof; for Frithiof I knew thee to be when first thou camest into my hall. Now stay with me, for my heart yearns towards thee and I am far stricken in years, and if thou wilt be my right hand for the days that are left, thou shalt have my land after my death for thine own."

But Frithiof shook his head sadly, saying: "not so, O king, for even now must I journey away from these shores."

Shortly after this Frithiof prepared to depart, and his dragon-ship lay at her moorings tugging as though eager to breast the waves of ocean once again. Then came he to Ring and Ingeborg, but the old king was at the point of death. "Valhalla calls to me," said he, "and my weary spirit wold fain be at rest. Frithiof, take thou my kingdom and guard the crown." He then placed the hand of his queen in that of Frithiof, and a moment later his spirit was borne by the Valkyrs into the Regions of the Blessed.

So they raised a mighty cairn above King Ring, and great was the mourning and lamentation in the land. Then all men looked to Frithiof as his successor, but he bade them give their allegiance to the son of King Ring, who was a right noble boy, and when they looked upon him they saw that he was worthy to wear his father's crown.

But because the people loved Frithiof, they cried: "Govern thou the realm while our king is young, and let us celebrate thy marriage with Ingeborg, as King Ring desired."

But Frithiof answered sadly: "I must fare over the seas to Balder's sacred grove. The mild god's wrath still burns against me. He took, he only can restore, my cherished bride."

The farewells have been spoken, the swift ship has cleaved the waves, and the hero stands in the desolate grove where once stood the temple of Balder, but where wild animals are now in hiding.

"Mild, blue-eyed Balder," speaks the hero, "will no atonement quit me of my guilt? Blood-fines take we for kinsmen slain, and the high gods are not wont to nurse their wrath when altar flames consume the sacrifice. Some offering ask, all that thou wilt is thine."

> "Then sudden, o'er the western waters pendent,
> An Image comes, with gold and flames resplendent,
> O'er Balder's grove it hovers, night's clouds under,
> Like gold crown resting on a bed of green.
> At last to a temple settling, firm 'tis grounded—
> Where Balder stood, another temple's founded."

Frithiof gazed in wonderment, and his heart went out in praise for the sign vouchsafed. He would raise a shrine more glorious than the one which had been destroyed by fire, and thus would he be at rest.

Now, while the timbers were being hewn and the carved pillars were taking shape, King Helge was absent upon a foray amongst the Finnish mountains. One day his band passed by a crag where stood the lonely shrine of some forgotten god, and King Helge scaled the rocky summit with intent to raze the ruined walls. The lock held fast and, as Helge tugged fiercely at the mouldered gate, suddenly a sculptured image of the deity, rudely summoned from his ancient sleep, started from his niche above.

Rudely he fell upon the head of the intruder, and Helge stretched his length upon the rocky floor, nor stirred again.

And now Balder's temple is finished, and its noble proportions look over the firth, in whose clear waters it is reflected. Its vast hall is filled melody, and the Chief Priest of Balder stands ready to receive a bride. But who stands frowning upon the threshold? King Halfdan it is, who approaches, sword in hand.

Frithiof with quick hands unbuckled the sword from his thigh and leaned it, with his golden shield, against the altar. Then with outstretched hand he advanced saying:

> "Most noble in this strife will he be found
> Who first is right hand good
> Offers in pledge of peaceful brotherhood."

Halfdan, blushing deeply, hastened to doff his iron gauntlet, and the two men, severed so long, forgot their enmity and pledged abiding faith with friendly grasp.

> "And as the last deep accents
> Of reconcilement sounded,
> Lo! Ingeborg sudden enters, rich adorn'd,
>   And to her brother's heart she trembling sinketh.
> He with his sister's fears
>   Deep-moved, her hand all tenderly in Frithiof's linketh,
> His burden soft transferring to the Hero's breast."

CHAPTER XXV

How the End of All Things Came About

*This is the tale the Northmen tell of how
the End of All Things Came About*

WHEN the Asa folk had banished wicked Loki to earth, and bound him fast in his gloomy cavern, they thought they had heard and seen the last of his evil ways.

But this was not to be the case. Finding he could not free himself, but must endure his bonds till the end of All Things, Loki tried to divert himself by enticing the earth people to him and teaching them to do every manner of evil. And so fast did knowledge of this evil spread, that the whole world soon became full of wickedness. Brothers fought and killed each other, men were for ever at war with other men, no one had time or room in his heart for pity or for kindliness.

So and Mani, who were wont to drive radiant through the sky in their golden chariots, grew pale with dismay, for they knew that these things portended their end, when those hungry wolves, who were ever pursuing them, would overtake and devour them utterly.

And they ceased to smile upon the land, wherefore the earth grew cold and dark, and a long, long winter began. From North, South, East, and West great snowstorms blew over the world, the Frost Giants waved their great wings and breathed an icy blast, and a thick layer of ice spread over the whole surface of the earth.

For six seasons this terrible winter held the world in its grip, and during all that time the earth people grew more wicked, until all traces of goodness disappeared. Meantime, deep down in the dark shades of the Ironwood, an evil Frost Giantess fed the pursuing wolves, so that they gained strength each day, and at length they were able to overtake Sol and Mani in their head-long course, and to devour them.

Now when that dreadful thing had happened, the whole earth shook to its foundations, and Loki, the Fenris Wolf, and the Sea-serpent, making one last tremendous effort, broke their bonds and rushed to wreak revenge upon their captors.

At that moment the dragon that lies at the root of the Tree of Life gnawed it through, so that it quivered and shook to its very top. The red cock who stood perched above the halls of Valhalla gave a shrill crow of alarm, and this was taken up by the white cock who roosts upon the tallest tree on the earth, and echoed by Hela's blood-red bird in the depths of the Mist Home.

Heimdall knew the meaning of these sounds, and putting the horn to his lips he gave the last long call from Asgard, which resounded across the Rainbow Bridge throughout the whole world.

Then the Asa folk sprang from their flower-strewn couches, and seizing their weapons, they mounted their battle steeds and rode across the Rainbow Bridge to the great plain where they were to wage their last fight.

Meantime, the Sea-serpent was lashing the waters of the ocean with his tail as he made his way through the blood-red waves to that dread battlefield. And Loki, who had roused all the host of the Fire Giants, was sailing thither as fast as the tossing ocean would carry his fatal barque; while from the foggy regions of the north issued the whole race of Frost Giants, eager for their revenge upon the hated Asa folk.

From a cleft in the earth came also Hela, the goddess of the underworld, followed by her gaunt watchdog and by all the evil dregs of her gloomy realm. Lastly, from a blinding flash of lightning that seemed to end the skies in twain, came forth the troop of Flame Giants, each with his fiery sword in hand.

Loki gladly placed himself at the head of all those hosts, and he led them forward boldly against the gods.

And first they thought to storm Asgard in one wild onset, but the Rainbow Bridge sank with a mighty crash under their horses' feet.

Meanwhile, the Asas had been gathering their forces upon the battlefield, where with calm, stern faces they awaited the attack of their foes—the red Flame Giants, the grim army of Hela, the grey-white host of the Frost Giants, led by Loki, with the Fenris Wolf on one hand and the Sea-serpent, breathing out clouds of deadly vapour, on the other.

> "And all are marshalled in one flaming square
> Against the gods, upon the plains of heaven."

Then came the crash of battle, in which, for all their courage, the Asas were bound to meet with defeat. Desperately they fought, but all to no avail, for, at the moment that Heimdall and Loki fell dead before each other's swords, and Thor, after killing the Sea-serpent, was drowned in the poisonous stream that flowed from the creature's mouth, the Fenris Wolf came at All-Father Odin with jaws open so wide that they reached from earth to heaven; and rushing upon the mighty Asa he engulfed him in that horrid tomb.

Most of the Asas, as well as their foes, now lay dead on the battlefield, and, seeing this, the Flame Giants suddenly grasped their fiery brands and flung them over earth and heaven and all the underworld.

The mighty Tree of Life withered and fell; the golden halls of Asgard melted away; the green things of earth turned black, and still the fire raged, until the whole world, burnt to a cinder, sank beneath the waves of the sea.

Thus did the End of All Things come about.

But because the End of All Things is also very often the Beginning of Others, the Northmen say that, after many long years, the old Earth rose again, clean and pure and bright from her long cleansing underneath the sea. And in the sky above a daughter of Sol again drove her sun-chariot, and smiled upon the earth, so that it grew young and fresh and green again.

And when this came to pass, a man and a woman, who, sunk in sleep in the depths of a forest, had escaped the universal destruction, came forth and took possession of the sweet green lands, for themselves and for their children for ever.

> "So perish the old Gods!
>   But out of the sea of Time
>   Rises a new land of song,
>   Fairer than the old.
>   Over is meadows green
>   Walk the young bards and sing.
>
>   Build it again,
>   O ye bards,
>   Fairer than before!

> Ye fathers of the new race,
> Feed upon morning dew,
> Sing the new Song of Love!
>
> The law of force is dead!
> The law of love prevails!
> Thor, the thunderer,
> Shall rule the earth no more,
> No more, with threats,
> Challenge the meek Christ.
>
> Sing no more,
> O ye bards of the North,
> Of Vikings and of Jarls!
> Of the days of Eld
> Preserve the freedom only,
> Not the deeds of blood."
>
> LONGFELLOW.

PRONOUNCING INDEX OF PROPER NAMES

(ā as in hate; ē as in tea; ō as in note; ä as in arm; ẽ as in merit)

Ægir (ā′jir)
Agnar (ag′nar)
Andvari (änd′vä-rē)
Angantyr (än-gän′tēr)
Angurvadel (än-gur-vä′del)
Angur-boda (än-gur-bō′dà)
Asa (ā′sa)
Asgard (as′gärd)
Ask (äsk)
Atli (at′lē)

Balder (baul′der)
Baugi (bow′gē)
Bele (bē-lā′)
Björn (byẽrn)
Bragi (brä′gē)
Branstock (bran′stok)
Bredi (bre′dē)
Brock (brock)
Brunhild (brōōn′hild)

Draupnir (drowp′nir)

Elli (el′lē)
Ellida (el-li′da)
Embla (em′bla)

Fafnir (faf′nir)
Fenga (fengá)
Fenris (fen′ris)
Fensalir (fen′säl-ir)
Fialar (fyäl′ar)
Fiorgyn (fyôr′gēn)

Frey (fri)
Freya (frī′a)
Frigga (frig′a)
Frithiof (frit′yof)

Galar (gäl′ar)
Geirrod (gir′rod)
Geri (gẽr′e)
Gersemi (gẽr′se-me)
Gialp (gyälp)
Gilling (gil′ling)
Giöll (gyẽl)
Giuki (gi′ōōki)
Gnomes (nōmz)
Greip (grīp)
Greyfell (grä-fel)
Grid (grēd)
Grimnir (grim′nir)
Grimhild (grim′hild)
Gudrun (goo′droon)
Gungnir (goong′nir)
Gunlod (goon′lod)
Gunnar (gun′när)
Guttorm (goot′torm)

Hamdir (ham′dir)
Halfdan (half′dan)
Heidrun (hi′drōōn)
Heimdall (hīm′däl)
Hela (helá)
Helge (hel′ge)
Hermod (hẽr′mod)
Hindfell (hind′fel)

Hiordis (hyôr´dis)

Hoder (hō´der)

Hœnir (hē´nir)

Högni (hēg´ne)

Hreidmar (hrīd´mar)

Hugi (hu´gi)

Hugin (hū´gin)

Hunding (hundíng)

Hyrroken (hēr´ro-kin)

Idun (ē´doon)

Ingeborg (in´ge-borg)

Jarl (yärl)

Kari (kär´ē)

Kvasir (kvä´sir)

Logi (lō´gē)

Loki (lō´kē)

Lygni (lēg´ni)

Mani (mä´nē)

Midgard (mid´gärd)

Mimir (mē´mir)

Miölnir (myēl´nir)

Modir (mō´dir)

Munin (mū´nin)

Niblungs (nē´bloongz)

Niffelheim (nĭf´l´hīm)

Niörd (nyērd)

Odin (ō´din)

Odur (ō´door)

Ragnarok (rag´na-ruk)

Ran (rän)

Ratatosk (rä´ta-tusk)

Rati (rä´tē)

Regin (rā´gin)

Rerir (rā´rir)

Ring (ring)

Ringhorn (ring´horn)

Roskva (ros´kva)

Sif (sif)

Siggeir (sig´īr)

Sigi (sig´ē)

Sigmund (sig´moond)

Signy (sig´ni)

Sigurd (sē´goord)

Sigyn (sē´gēn)

Sindri (sin´drē)

Sinfiotli (sin-fe-ot´li)

Skadi (skä´dē)

Skrymir (skrim´ir)

Sleipnir (slīp´nir)

Sol (sōl)

Suttung (soot´tōōng)

Svadilfare (svä´dil-fär´e)

Thialfi (te´älf´e)

Thiassi (te-äs-se)

Thok (tok)

Thor (thor or tor)

Thorsten (tor-sten)

Thrym (trim)

Tyr (tēr)

Uplands (up´lands)

Valhalla (väl-häl´la)

Vali (väl´ē)

Valkyrs (val´kirz)

Valtam (väl´tam)

Vikings (vik´ingz)

Volsung (vol´soong)

Ymir (ē´mir)